Contents

Introduction

Teacher Quality and Educational Equity

By Caroline Chauncey

Since the enactment of the No Child Left Behind Act in January 2002, a "perfect storm" has converged over teacher quality in education. Three slow-brewing trends —the graying of the teaching force, the increase in school enrollments, and the high rate of attrition among new teachers—collided with the federally legislated mandate to ensure that there is a "highly qualified" teacher in every classroom by the 2005–06 school year. Although the definition of "highly qualified" remains conveniently nebulous, the underlying pressure on school administrators to recruit, retain, and support qualified teachers is mounting. And for good reason.

A growing body of research shows that teacher quality has an enormous impact on student learning—more than class size, more than per-pupil spending, more than the child's socioeconomic background or previous academic performance. Yet many of our nation's children spend long hours in classrooms where teachers are inexperienced, untrained, or academically unprepared. About 40 percent of middle school students, for instance, have at least one teacher who hasn't even minored in the subject he or she is teaching. For high school students, the figure is 25 percent—and for high school students in high-poverty schools, it's almost one-third.

Students in high-poverty schools also suffer disproportionately from high rates of teacher turnover. By one estimate, these schools lose as much as one-fifth of their teaching staff each year. And they often have the hardest time finding qualified replacements. Teachers in these schools are disproportionately likely to be novices with less than three years' experience, to be teaching on emergency waivers, or to be uncertified in the subjects they teach. Clearly, unequal access to qualified teachers is one of the key factors contributing to the achievement gap in American education.

Over the last several years, the *Harvard Education Letter* has devoted substantial coverage to the issue of teacher quality. This latest volume in the *Harvard Education Letter* Spotlight Series presents eight previously published articles along with four additional chapters newly commissioned for this collection. Together, they offer an overview of the historical and cultural factors that have contributed to this "perfect storm" in the teaching profession and frame the debate over its future. And they provide a variety of strategies for principals and other administrators to use to improve the quality of teaching in their schools—from identifying and hiring talented candidates to building the institutional relationships that support professional growth for novice and experienced teachers alike.

In the opening chapter, Pam Grossman traces the 20-year legacy of *A Nation at Risk*, the 1983 report by the National Commission on Excellence in Education. She shows how its predictions of an impending teacher shortage laid the groundwork for a series of reforms that eased entry into the profession and established a trend toward the deskilling and deprofessionalization of teaching. This theme is taken up in chapter 2 by Katherine C. Boles and Vivian Troen, who set out a model for making teaching a profession—not merely a job. They argue that the culture of isolationism and egalitarianism within schools undermines efforts to attract more qualified and capable candidates, foster their professional growth, and hold them accountable for student learning. In the interview that follows, Katherine K. Merseth reflects on how teacher-education programs can better prepare young teachers for the realities of teaching in urban schools—and what school administrators can do to make the profession more appealing.

Taking the administrator's perspective, chapters 4 and 5 address the challenges of identifying and hiring the most effective teachers. In chapter 4, Robert Rothman outlines the research that tells principals what to look for in the search for talented teachers and surveys a variety of innovative hiring strategies designed to ensure a good fit between the prospective teacher and the school. In chapter 5, Debra Viadero discusses the pros and cons of hiring teachers who come to the classroom through alternative-certification programs—and punctures some of the myths about who those teachers are.

A key theme that runs through the literature on teacher quality is the importance of providing support for novice teachers. Reino Makkonen's chapter summarizes the research on attrition among new teachers, identifying causes that range from discipline problems to career aspirations, and surveys a range of strategies schools can use to improve working conditions for all teachers. The chapters that follow explore some of these strategies in greater depth. In chapter 7, Susan M. Kardos documents the growth of induction programs for new teachers and analyzes the elements critical for their success. In chapter 8, Morgaen L. Donaldson discusses the re-emergence of career ladders for teachers, a reform that withered on the vine in the 1980s but appears to be enjoying new vitality—in part, as an unexpected offshoot of the movement toward standards-based accountability.

One example of the effort to create upward mobility within the teaching career is the use of formal certification to identify highly skilled teachers. In chapter 9, David T. Gordon examines the rigorous requirements for certification by the National Board for Professional Teaching Standards and discusses the impact of national board certification on teacher performance, student learning, and the profession as a whole. Another emerging strategy for fostering professional growth among veteran as well as novice teachers is school-based coaching, which Alexander Russo discusses in chapter 10. He traces the growing popularity of this intervention and outlines the challenges schools must face—logistical, financial, and cultural—to ensure that coaching is effective.

The final chapters of the book examine how the emphasis on teacher quality is placing new demands on today's principals. In chapter 11, Louise Kennedy speaks with principals about the thorny issue of teacher evaluation and gathers tips on making it a collaborative process. And in chapter 12, Alexander Russo analyzes the need for new skills among school leaders and describes innovative recruitment and training programs aimed to help principals succeed in their new roles.

Together, this collection of essays outlines the key challenges facing today's principals and administrators in the effort to develop and strengthen the caliber of teaching in their schools. More important, these chapters point the way to the kinds of changes educators can make—school by school, district by district, state by state—to ensure that all children have access to highly qualified teachers and that teaching as a profession is able to attract and keep talented, skilled, and dedicated teachers who can open the doors of discovery and opportunity for every child.

CHAPTER 1

Teaching:
From *A Nation at Risk*
to a Profession at Risk?

By Pam Grossman

Despite all of the educational reform activity over the past two decades, the teaching profession currently faces daunting challenges. These include the influx of underqualified teachers into classrooms, the potential dismantling of professional education for teachers, and the trend toward the regulation of teaching practice—regulations that may deprive teachers of the ability to make professional judgments and exercise their professional knowledge. So we face a paradox: in some areas teachers are better prepared than ever, while in schools that serve the greatest numbers of poor and minority children, more and more teachers are underqualified. Due in part to the reforms enacted in response to *A Nation at Risk*, it is harder than ever to get into a teacher-education program. But in many communities, individuals can bypass these requirements altogether and enter the classroom with an emergency credential.

Beginning with the publication of *A Nation at Risk*, reports began to warn of impending teacher shortages.[1] Due to increases in both student enrollment and teacher retirements, widespread shortages were predicted, particularly in the areas of special education, English as a Second Language, math, and science. At least partly in response to the increasing demand for teachers and fears of teacher shortages, states began to issue emergency credentials and create alternate routes into teaching. In 1996, the National Commission on Teaching and America's Future demonstrated the prevalence of the practice of staffing schools with teachers who did not hold full qualifications in their field. The commission's study reported that as of 1996, "more than 50,000 people who lack the training required for their jobs have entered teaching annually on emergency or substandard license."[2] These numbers have only increased since then. One 2002 study of California suggests that half of all first-year teachers do not have their credentials when they begin teaching.[3]

A standard response to teacher shortages has always been to ease entry into the profession. Such a response diminishes the need to keep salaries competitive in order to attract promising candidates and provide an incentive for investing in professional preparation. In keeping with this tradition, the Bush administration is calling the entire enterprise of teacher education into question, citing the shortage of qualified teachers. In the 2002 report, "Meeting the Highly Qualified Teacher Challenge," the U.S. Secretary of Education essentially calls for the abolition of professional education as it currently exists. The report concludes that states should cease requiring traditional teacher education. Instead, "states will need to streamline their certification system to focus on the few things that really matter: verbal ability, content knowledge, and, as a safety precaution, a background check of new teachers."[4]

Since one of the hallmarks of a profession is a specialized body of knowledge acquired through professional education, such a proposal strikes at the heart of the claim that teaching be considered a profession. The proposal also ignores research indicating that courses in how to teach a subject contribute more to a teacher's success than additional subject-matter courses.[5] Without professional preparation, prospective teachers forgo opportunities to develop knowledge of how to teach reading or math, knowledge of how students develop and learn—all topics that are generally covered in the professional component of the teacher education curriculum.

I recently watched a film entitled *The First Year*. It highlights the experience of five first-year teachers in Los Angeles. One of the story lines follows a deeply committed young man as he tries to arrange for speech therapy for one of his students. The teacher is shown working individually with the student (one of the few scenes of actual instruction shown in the movie). The teacher patiently tries to get the student to sound out the word two—/t/ /wh/ /oo/. For all his good intentions, energy, and commitment, this teacher, who entered teaching through Teach for America, did not know the difference between phonetically regular words, such as cat or three, which students should be encouraged to sound out, and phonetically irregular words, like two, which are generally taught as high-frequency sight words.

Because teaching reading is complex, courses in teaching reading are required at virtually all accredited teacher-education programs. One of the other committed young teachers, another Teach For America member, attended the screening of the movie. Following the film, she was asked what she wished she had known before she entered the classroom. She said she was unprepared to teach reading to the large numbers of her middle school students who were unable to read at grade level. Based on her experience, she had applied to the teacher-education program at Mills College and was about to graduate soon after the screening. She proudly announced that she now felt prepared to teach reading to her future students.

A Nation at Risk recognized the need both to raise admission standards for applicants to teacher-education programs and to strengthen the quality of the programs themselves. To dismantle university-based teacher education, rather than to invest in the improvement of teachers' professional education and development, would deprive prospective teachers of the opportunity to develop the understanding of how to teach challenging subject matter to all students, a key component of the reform effort. Such a direction would also undermine the effort to make teaching more professional.

WORKING CONDITIONS

While proposals to ease entry into teaching have been based on claims of teacher shortages, others have argued that the problem is not a shortage of teachers, except in a few areas. Rather, high teacher turnover, particularly in challenging schools, creates the continual demand for new teachers. From this perspective, teacher retention, rather than teacher supply, is the culprit. Retention of new teachers, in turn, is directly linked to the working conditions. In an organizational analysis of teacher shortages, Richard Ingersoll of the University of Pennsylvania argues that organizational features of schools help account for higher or lower rates of teacher turnover: "The data show, in particular, that inadequate support from the school administration, student discipline problems, limited faculty input into school decisionmaking, and, to a lesser extent, low salaries are all associated with higher rates of turnover, after controlling for the characteristics of both teachers and schools."[6]

Ingersoll's analysis supports the need to create more supportive working conditions for teachers, which includes allowing teachers to influence decisions that affect their classrooms—a recommendation of *A Nation at Risk* as well. He suggests that the schools with the highest turnover are least well equipped to support beginning teachers.

A key recommendation of *A Nation at Risk* was the need to create better working conditions for teachers, conditions that would attract and retain promising candidates into the profession. Such working conditions include competitive salaries, opportunities to engage in professional development, and a voice in decisions that affect their practice. How far have we come in meeting this recommendation?

While there has been some progress in raising teacher salaries over the past two decades, by and large teacher salaries nationwide have not kept up with inflation. A 2002 report by the National Center for Education Statistics found that, after adjusting for inflation, teachers' salaries actually declined 1 percent between 1990–91 and 2000–01.[7] The pressure to raise salaries has been tempered by the political exigency of hiring teachers who are not fully certified. Partly because of the failure to raise salaries, teaching as a career option continues to compete with other much more lucrative careers that also require a college degree, while standards for entry into the profession are being lowered in response to teacher shortages.

A Nation at Risk also highlighted the need to create more challenging career opportunities for teachers, and many more opportunities for teacher leadership exist today. The National Board for Professional Teaching Standards represents only one example of an organization that recognizes teachers' accomplishments. As of mid-2002, the Board had certified 16,044 teachers across the nation (see chapter 9). These teachers work intensively to document their classroom practice and prepare portfolios that demonstrate the accomplishments and learning of their students. Across the country, Board-certified teachers have begun to take on positions of leadership in education and to participate actively in school reform, teacher education, and professional development. The accomplishments of these teachers represent the best of the profession, the path we could choose to take in meeting the challenge of finding highly qualified teachers. As a group, they demonstrate how investing in teachers' professional knowledge and development can pay off, not only in the classroom but in the profession as a whole.

TOWARD THE REGULATION OF TEACHING PRACTICE

Due in large part to the confluence of increased accountability measures, including high-stakes standardized assessments and the influx of both new and underqualified teachers into schools, districts around the country have begun to invest heavily in a variety of scripted curriculum materials. Many see this move as contributing to the deskilling of teachers and the deprofessionalization of teaching. Nowhere is this debate more evident than in teachers' responses to district-mandated programs such as Open Court for teaching reading.

According to a 2002 issue of *California Educator* devoted to this topic, the Open Court curriculum had been adopted by one in eight elementary schools in California by the year 2000.[8] While there are undoubtedly many strengths in the curriculum as originally designed, with its emphasis on phonemic awareness and support for early decoding skills among beginning readers, it is also highly prescriptive; teachers must follow a set time frame and script for instruction. Teachers have complained that the program robs them of the ability to tailor instruction to their particular group of students. One teacher in Los Angeles, a district that has invested heavily in the program, was told he must stop teaching Shakespeare to his elementary school students in order to teach Open Court, despite the success of his students on reading assessments.

On the one hand, requiring such scripted programs is a logical response to the rising numbers of new and underprepared teachers in the schools. Even well-prepared novices need well-designed curriculum materials to succeed, and new teachers who have little background in the teaching of reading would need even more guidance. But substituting programmed materials for investment in teacher knowledge and judgment is a shortsighted solution to a long-term problem. Such a solution will only further decrease the attractiveness of teaching to the kinds of individuals the Department of Education hopes to lure into the classroom with reduced entry requirements. At the other end of the career spectrum, highly accomplished teachers may find themselves increasingly stymied in their efforts to meet the needs of individual children, as was true of the Los Angeles teacher fighting to keep Shakespeare in his curriculum.

INEQUITY

An especially troubling consequence of the failure to professionalize teaching is that students in low-income and high-minority schools are much more likely to have less-qualified teachers.[9] In California alone, as of 1999, 11 percent of teachers were on emergency permits or waivers, with the majority of these teachers concentrated in high-poverty districts. Another report on the status of the teaching profession in California found that in schools with the highest percentage of students qualifying for free or reduced-price lunch, 22 percent of teachers were underqualified, while in schools with the lowest percentage of such students, only 6 percent of teachers were underqualified.[10] The New York Regents Task Force on Teaching reported that 12 percent of teachers in schools with the highest number of minority students were not certified in the field they teach, compared to only 5.4 percent in the schools with the lowest percentage of minority students.[11]

Twenty years ago, we learned from *A Nation at Risk* that we were metaphorically at war; 20 years later, teachers are still fighting for professional recognition and respect. At a time when we have more evidence than ever that quality teaching matters enormously to children's futures, we are on the verge of forsaking the hard-won reforms that can lead to better prepared teachers for all students. The crossroad is clearly marked. We can continue to invest in the development of highly qualified and well-prepared teachers and create the incentives and working conditions to keep them in the profession. Or we can once again ease standards for entry into teaching and allow students, primarily those in high-poverty schools who are most in need of high-quality teaching, to be taught by less than qualified teachers. To pursue the latter path would only increase the disparities in educational opportunity and achievement that already exist within our society. The nation, and the teaching profession, remains at risk.

This chapter originally appeared in the January/February 2003 issue of the Harvard Education Letter.

NOTES

1. See Linda Darling-Hammond, *Beyond the Commission Reports* (Santa Monica, CA: Rand Corporation, 1984); also Richard J. Murnane, Judith D. Singer, John D. Willett, James J. Kemple, and Randall J. Olsen, *Who Will Teach? Policies That Matter* (Cambridge, MA: Harvard University Press, 1991).

2. National Commission on Teaching and America's Future, *What Matters Most: Teaching for America's Future* (New York: Author, 1996), p. 15.

3. See *Teaching and California's Future: The Status of the Teaching Profession 2001* (Santa Cruz, CA: Center for the Future of Teaching and Learning, 2002).

4. U.S. Department of Education, *Meeting the Highly Qualified Teacher Challenge: The Secretary's Annual Report on Teacher Quality* (Washington, DC: U.S. Government Printing Office, 2002), p. 40.

5. For an overview of this research, see Suzanne M. Wilson, Robert E. Floden, and Joan Ferrini-Mundy, *Teacher Preparation Research: Current Knowledge, Gaps, and Recommendations* (Seattle: Center for the Study of Teaching and Policy, University of Washington, 2001).

6. Richard M. Ingersoll, "Teacher Turnover and Teacher Shortages: An Organizational Analysis," *American Education Research Journal* 38, no. 3 (2001), 501.

7. National Center for Education Statistics: Elementary and Secondary Education (ch. 2). http://nces.ed.gov/pubs2002/2002130b.pdf

8. See "Scripted Learning: A Slap in the Face or Blessing from Above?" *California Educator,* April 2002.

9. See Hamilton Lankford, Susanna Loeb, and James Wyckoff, "Teacher Sorting and the Plight of Urban Schools: A Descriptive Analysis," *Educational Evaluation and Policy Analysis* 24, no. 1 (2002), 37–62; Stephen W. Raudenbush, Randall P. Fotiu, and Yuk Fai Cheong, "Inequality of Access to Educational Resources: A National Report Card in 8th Grade Math," *Educational Evaluation and Policy Analysis* 20, no. 4 (1998), 253–267.

10. See *Teaching and California's Future: The Status of the Teaching Profession 2001.*

11. Regents Task Force on Teaching, *Teaching to Higher Standards: New York's Commitment* (Albany: New York State Department of Education, 1998), p. 10.

CHAPTER 2

Mamas, Don't Let Your Babies Grow Up to Be Teachers

School reforms are destined to fail until teaching becomes a professional career

By Katherine C. Boles and Vivian Troen

It is telling that an American parent's aspirations for a son or daughter often include the practice of medicine or law but almost never of education. An African American student at Harvard told us her parents tried to discourage her from becoming a teacher. They advised her to go into some other field where, as a smart and talented young woman, she "could be a real success." She went into teaching despite the urgings of her parents and many of her friends. She is an exception—one of the few academically accomplished college students who choose teaching over other, more attractive opportunities.

Teaching is a job—not a profession or even a career. There are recognized criteria, after all, for a profession, and teaching meets almost none of them (see chart, p. 20). And for a job to be a career, there must be a visible and attainable career ladder with advancements based on increased experience, knowledge, and expertise.

To understand the deficiencies of this job-that-is-not-a-professional-career, we must look at teaching's history. In the industrialized 19th century, women, recently freed from farm work by mechanization, took up the only intellectual jobs available to them. By 1885, women made up 90 percent of the teaching force (a ratio almost the same in elementary schools today), working in poor conditions for little pay. In the 20th century, once women obtained the right and the means to compete for nearly any job available to men, fewer chose teaching. The shortage of qualified classroom teachers is now a national crisis. Although a softening of the economy and a shortage of jobs have many college grads considering teaching, most see this as a short-term option. When they find the positions they really want, they'll quickly leave.

To find long-term solutions to the teacher crisis, we must take off the blinders and look at the system as a whole. Public education suffers under what we call a Trilemma Dysfunction—a three-component cycle that stymies effective education reform:

- Not enough academically able candidates are attracted to teaching.
- Teacher-education programs do an inadequate job of preparing classroom teachers.
- The professional work life of the teacher is, on the whole, unacceptable.

First identified in *A Nation at Risk*, this is a self-perpetuating cycle—one in which the underqualified are given inadequate preparation to enter a workplace culture that defeats attempts at excellence. It is highly resistant to the kinds of systemic changes needed for the improvement of public education. And it is the primary reason why most proposed reforms, even those that would make sense if they could be implemented, are doomed to fail.

How to break the cycle of dysfunction? If a magic wand could make every student entering a teacher-preparation program the perfect candidate for classroom teaching, it still would not solve the problem, because even the best students would be stymied by the poor education they receive at most graduate schools. Wave the wand again to upgrade every teacher-preparation program in the country and the cycle would still not be broken.

Why? Because the true culprit in the equation is the nonprofessional culture of classroom teaching (see box, p. 20). It is there that the pursuit of educational improvement is defeated and it is there that the work must begin.

EQUAL AND ISOLATED

Based on a model of industrialization that viewed teachers as interchangeable assembly-line workers, teaching is both egalitarian and isolationist. Egalitarianism is the pervasive myth that every teacher is as good as every other teacher. The flat organizational structure, with one principal at the top and all teachers on one level underneath, effectively squashes attempts at leadership and true professional development. This is a neat organizational/cultural device for keeping each teacher in her place. Should one teacher aspire to improve her practice, she must do it quietly, alone, and preferably unnoticed— or run the risk of being labeled and ostracized.

NOT A PROFESSION	A PROFESSION
Egalitarianism—no career ladder	Recognition for achievement—clearly defined career path
Isolation—practice is a freelance craft	Practice characterized by teamwork and collaboration
Poor preparation—"anybody can do it"	Rigorous educational standards and required skills
Little or no mentoring	Mentoring is the norm
Weak professional development	Professional development integral to the career
Practice not based on research	Research informs practice
Lack of accountability	Everyone accountable
Bottom of the power structure	Shared decisionmaking

Combined with egalitarianism, isolationism makes collaboration with peers virtually impossible and keeps teaching a private act. This effectively defeats attempts at accountability, because supervision and mentoring, while given lip service, are never well implemented. Teachers who ask for help are treated as incompetent, and the very notion of an "equal" teacher giving advice to another teacher who is already supposed to know everything she needs to know is seen as patently ridiculous. For the same reason, schools currently putting teachers in "teams" are merely engaged in a game of rearranging chairs because, of course, teams without acknowledged leaders are mostly ineffective.

We will not see long-lasting improvement in overall educational quality until we reinvent the job of teaching as a true profession—transforming an isolated, freelance culture in which mediocrity is the norm into an open, collaborative culture that fosters excellence and accountability.

A MULTITIERED PROFESSION

The first task in the professionalization of teaching is to create a career ladder—a multitiered structure in which different teachers have different job descriptions and responsibilities. We have imagined schools in which the principal supervises not 70 or 80 teachers and paraprofessionals, but a cadre of perhaps four chief instructors. Each chief instructor in turn supervises and is responsible for the performance of perhaps two teams, each made up of professional teachers, fully licensed teachers, associate teachers, and teaching interns.

Teaching interns are graduate or undergraduate students who work full-time in classrooms as part of a degree-granting program with a university. They are not on the fringe of the school but are considered junior faculty who have responsibilities for the instruction of children. This includes classroom teaching responsibilities part of the time, under the close supervision of a professional teacher.

Associate teachers are the novices, first-time teachers who are participating in an intensive two-year period of induction. Rather than flying solo, they teach classes only part of the week as they receive constant supervision and mentoring. At the end of two years they become fully licensed teachers and, if they wish, advance their careers to the level of professional teacher or chief instructor.

Chief instructors are the team leaders who supervise teams consisting of professional teachers, fully licensed teachers, associate teachers, and interns. The chief instructor earns a credential by working several years as a professional teacher, plus intensive study; the position offers the highest pay and the highest level of achievement in the teaching profession. A chief instructor must be an expert in content, curriculum development, student learning and assessment, and must demonstrate the ability to translate relevant and proven research into practice. The chief instructor must also provide tangible evidence of contributions to the profession, including research, publications, university teaching, and/or presentations at conferences. Working an 11-month year, the chief instructor's primary responsibilities are supervision and mentoring—assisting colleagues, giving demonstration lessons, observing, coaching, and facilitating curriculum and staff development.

This model is designed not only to transform the profession but also the culture, making commonplace that which was formerly impossible. An open system where everyone's work is visible leads to accountability for everyone. Under the leadership of a principal who has been schooled in this new form of power sharing, true teamwork and collaboration lead to shared decisionmaking and the improvement of individual practice. Mentoring, supervision, and professional development are no longer "add-ons" but integral components of the career. A clearly defined career path provides tangible rewards for accomplishment and professional recognition.

When teaching becomes a *real* profession, more academically able people will be drawn into it (and stay), colleges will be forced by market competition to improve the quality of their education, and better prepared teachers will enter the classroom and improve the profession.

As Larry Cuban and David Tyack have pointed out, Americans are fond of constantly tinkering to improve education. Well, we've seen the results of tinkering on scales both grand and small, and it isn't a pretty picture. It's time to stop tinkering and do the serious work necessary to transform and professionalize teaching once and for all. We'll know we've been successful when mamas again want their babies to grow up to be teachers.

This chapter originally appeared in the September/October 2003 issue of the Harvard Education Letter.

FOR FURTHER INFORMATION

R.S. Barth. *Improving Schools from Within*. San Francisco, CA: Jossey-Bass, 1990.

N. Hoffman. *Woman's "True" Profession: Voices from the History of Teaching* (2nd ed.) Cambridge, MA: Harvard Education Press, 2003.

National Commission on Excellence in Education. *A Nation at Risk: The Imperative for Educational Reform*. Washington, DC: U.S. Department of Education, 1983.

J.D. Saphier. *Bonfires and Magic Bullets: Making Teaching a True Profession, the Step Without Which Other Reforms Will Never Take nor Endure*. Carlisle, MA: Research for Better Teaching, 1995.

V. Troen and K.C. Boles. *Who's Teaching Your Children? Why the Teacher Crisis Is Worse Than You Think and What Can Be Done About It*. New Haven, CT: Yale University Press, 2003.

D.B. Tyack. *The One Best System: A History of American Urban Education*. Cambridge, MA: Harvard University Press, 1974.

D. Tyack and L. Cuban. *Tinkering Toward Utopia: A Century of Public School Reform*. Cambridge, MA: Harvard University Press, 1995.

CHAPTER 3

Arming New Teachers with Survival Skills

A conversation with Katherine K. Merseth

Katherine K. Merseth is director of the Teacher Education Program at the Harvard Graduate School of Education, a program she founded in 1983. Her charge: to prepare teachers to work in urban schools in an era of standards-based reform and tougher accountability for teachers. She spoke with the Harvard Education Letter *about what that challenge entails.*

How can teacher ed programs make the profession more appealing to young teachers?

We need to find more ways to emphasize leadership and arm new teachers with the skills to become change agents. Simply putting well-trained, competent teachers in dysfunctional schools is a recipe for disaster. They'll leave. Fifty percent leave in five years, and everybody scratches their heads and wonders why. Money is important, but it's not the reason that people leave. They come into the profession believing that they can make a real difference, but the bureaucratic obstacles they face seem insurmountable.

What are some survival skills new teachers need?

Teachers must reflect on their practice and make that a habit. Teacher research is important if they are to really understand the situations they're in. Also, they need to understand school reform strategies—what's been tried, what's worked, what hasn't, and what could work in the future. By doing so, they will begin to understand why they're making progress on a problem—or not.... And of course, teachers have to become effective pedagogues with a whole repertoire of skills.

Critics of ed schools say that teacher training should focus less on pedagogy and more on content—that if teachers knew the content, the pedagogy would take care of itself. How would you respond?

Teachers do need that fundamental content knowledge. But they also need to be able to understand how children learn, the different points of view, perceptions, conceptions, and understandings that they bring to learning. It's important to have techniques in your repertoire for understanding the way kids make sense of things.

Can you explain to me why one-half divided by two-thirds is three-fourths? Don't tell me how to do it, because that's what many people will do. Give me an example. Tell me a story that represents that equation. Explain why it works the way it does. We all know you invert and multiply. But why? Or as a kid once said, "If x equals five, why did you call it x? Why didn't you just call it five?"

There are instances where you need to be able to think like a kid. You also need to be able to draw on the content knowledge itself. There are plenty of people teaching mathematics in particular who don't have the content background. But that's not to say that simply having the content background will make you an effective teacher. You've got to have both content and approach.

So learning how to get to know kids is an important part of teacher ed?

You bet! In order to be an effective teacher, you must understand your audience. You must understand the kids that are sitting in front of you. Kids aren't empty vessels that we just pour information into. That's the old model. In this world of increasing diversity and increasing accountability, we can't afford to have kids not "get it."

So a key piece of teaching is being able to read your students, differentiate your instruction based on your assessment of the individual kids, and develop 14 different ways to talk about how to factor an equation. Some kids will learn best visually. Others will learn best with words. Others learn best by talking with a peer. They may speak different languages than many of our teachers do. They may come from different socioeconomic and home situations than our teachers do. So understanding students is a challenge that is critically important.

When you talk about the importance of teacher research, are you saying that teachers need to put more effort into reading and understanding existing research or that they need to do research themselves in their own classrooms?

Both. They need to be able to look at a piece of research and say, "What does this mean for me and my classroom?" But the power and stimulus for change will come when teachers better understand what's happening in their own classrooms.

Traditionally, we haven't helped teachers know how to do that. If only one out of nine kids did their assignment for today, you can throw your hands up and say, "These darn kids." Or you can say, "Now, I wonder what this is all about. And how would I find out for sure?" That's what enables teachers to have some control over their lives. Young teachers think, "There's nothing I can do. I can't change my principal. I can't change the bureaucracy. I can't change these kids. I don't understand." Teacher research is a way of gaining some control and some power over your situation.

How can preservice learning facilitate this?

I am a huge proponent of practice-based learning from the first day. To stand in front of a classroom of kids has a way of focusing your thinking and grounding your experience. Then everything you try to do is in the service of the question of how this plays in the real world, rather than what contribution this makes to the literature.

What does reflective practice entail?

Having the time, the opportunity, and the skills to really ask hard questions about your classroom, your instruction, and your kids. Having the skill and the time to document what you know and don't know, what you want to know, and how you might find it out. But it's not only reflecting on your practice in an external way but in an internal way, too. What do you believe to be the purpose of education? What do you believe is your mission in being a teacher in the school?

I can't tell you how many teachers I've asked to finish the sentence "Curriculum is..." who say, "You know, I never thought of that before." One reason schools have such a hard time with reform is that people do not articulate what they believe. People end up working at cross purposes because they have fundamentally different views about why we educate children, but they keep all that hidden. These deeply held beliefs about purpose are huge and become evident in remarkably counterproductive ways.

It sounds like you want teachers to take charge of their own professional development.

I'm reminded of the Debbie Meier quote, "Show me a school where teachers are learning, and I'll show you a school where kids are learning." A principal should encourage investigation, inquiry, exploration, and ownership of the knowledge—just as teachers should encourage these things in kids. For something to stick, you have to do it. You have to experience it yourself. Teachers have for too long felt that they have no control. In fact, they have a huge amount of control.

From the administrator's point of view, there's the delicate balance that [NYU education professor] Joe McDonald talks about: How much clutch and how much gas? How much freedom do I give? What do I have to decide and what is best left for teachers to decide?

What should an administrator look for in a job candidate who's new to teaching?

The first thing, obviously, is whether they have the content and pedagogical knowledge they need. I would take a topic in their field and ask them to explain it to me, keeping an eye out for how they communicate and connect. Second, can they collaborate with others? We all know of plenty of superstars who don't do much for the rest of the building. In hiring, I would look for someone who values collaboration and works well with others. Third, are they someone who has the ability to reflect on what they are doing—to think about and change their practice with a can-do attitude?

What can an administrator do to keep and support them?

Before they make any decision within administrative roles, they should be able to answer the question, "What does this have to do with teaching and learning?" They need to realize that the core enterprise of this business is teaching and learning. It's not child care. It's not transportation. It's not food services. It's not dealing with the Department of Social Services. It's teaching and learning. Administrators who make that commitment first will go a long way toward retaining the best teachers.

A shorter version of this interview originally appeared in the September/ October 2002 issue of the Harvard Education Letter.

CHAPTER 4

Landing the "Highly Qualified Teacher"

How administrators can hire—and keep—the best

By Robert Rothman

Applicants for teaching positions at Blue Creek Elementary School in the North Colonie (N.Y.) School District go through a grueling process. First, a team assembled from all six elementary schools in the district screens their applications, looking at their college grade-point averages, the rigor of the courses they took, their extracurricular activities, and their experience working with diverse students, among other factors. Promising applicants are then invited for interviews.

The interview process is "overwhelming" for the candidates, according to Rose Jackson, Blue Creek's principal. In all, six principals, an assistant superintendent, two or three parents, and two or three students quiz prospective teachers on instructional issues, such as classroom management strategies and ideas for using technology. And that's not all. "If we have the opportunity—we don't do it as much as we'd

31

like—we observe the teacher or invite them to do a model lesson," says Jackson. "That's been successful for us, although it is stressful for the candidates."

The process at Blue Creek is unusually thorough. Because the district, which is located outside of Albany, attracts 200 to 300 applicants for every elementary teaching position, principals like Jackson can select from a variety of competitive candidates. In addition, the screening process eliminates the central office bottlenecks that often plague large districts, particularly urban districts, which in many cases hire teachers close to—or after—the start of the school year and have a limited pool from which to draw. Few schools conduct the intense interviews and teacher observations that Blue Creek does.

Yet even Jackson worries that the North Colonie process may not be perfect in matching applicants to positions. The initial screening of paper credentials might weed out an excellent prospective teacher, she notes. "The best candidate for us might be one we turned down," Jackson says.

THE RESEARCH: TEACHING COUNTS

Although the process of hiring workers is a challenge in any industry, the stakes of getting it right in education are particularly high. A growing body of research suggests strongly that the quality of teaching is the largest school-related factor associated with student achievement. Studies conducted in Tennessee, Dallas, and elsewhere have shown that good teachers can improve student achievement by as much as an extra grade level over the course of a year.

Moreover, the effects of teacher quality are cumulative. Researchers from the Dallas Independent School District found that students assigned for three years in a row to effective teachers—those whose students gained in achievement more than would be expected by past performance—went from the 59th percentile in the fourth grade to the 76th percentile in the sixth. But a similar group of students assigned to less effective teachers actually lost ground over that period: they went from the 60th percentile to the 42nd.

The Tennessee study, which examined the "value added" that teachers provide, showed that even low-achieving students of the most effective teachers gained about three times as much in achievement as those taught by the least effective teachers.

Reflecting such findings, the No Child Left Behind Act, the 2001 reauthorization of the Elementary and Secondary Education Act, requires schools to employ "highly qualified teachers" in every classroom. Under the law, all teachers in public schools must be highly qualified by 2005–06.

Although the law allows states to come up with their own definitions of "highly qualified," the U.S. Department of Education requires that, at a minimum, such teachers have a four-year college degree, a full state teaching license, and demonstrated knowledge of the subject they are teaching, either by having a college major in the subject or by passing an examination.

WHO *IS* THE EFFECTIVE TEACHER?

There is little research on the characteristics of effective teachers—perhaps surprising, given the growing recognition of the importance of teaching. One recent synthesis, conducted by Jennifer King Rice, an associate professor of educational policy and leadership at the University of Maryland, found that teachers' years of experience, the selectivity of the college or university they attended, whether they held a certificate in the subject they taught, their coursework in subject matter and pedagogy, and their verbal abilities (as measured by tests like the SAT) were all associated with higher levels of student achievement. By contrast, there was little evidence of the impact on student achievement of emergency certification or scores on teacher licensing tests.

However, the study also found large gaps in the research. There is little research, for example, on teacher quality in elementary and middle schools, in subjects other than mathematics, and for teachers of special populations, such as English-language learners or students with disabilities.

Nevertheless, the research does suggest some factors principals can look for in hiring teachers, Rice says. Subject-area knowledge is important, and an undergraduate major in the subject taught is a useful clue, particularly for high school mathematics teachers. But "advanced degrees don't seem to matter much, unless you pay close attention to the alignment of what teachers teach and what is learned in the higher degree programs," she says. On the other hand, knowledge of pedagogy is crucial. "I would be reluctant to hire anyone with no experience or no coursework in teaching methods," Rice says.

In an effort to codify these types of factors, a new organization, the American Board for Certification of Teacher Excellence (ABCTE), is developing a test that will be administered nationwide and will offer certificates to any prospective teacher who passes it, regardless of whether or not the candidate attended a teacher-education institution. The board's certificate has been adopted in Pennsylvania, and the U.S. Department of Education recently awarded the organization a $35 million grant to expand its development efforts. [As of September 2004, Pennsylvania, Idaho, Florida, and New Hampshire had approved the board certificate.] The ABCTE is also developing a certification for experienced teachers that would compete with the National Board for Professional Teaching Standards (see chapter 9).

Kathleen Madigan, president of the ABCTE, says the test reflects the concerns of principals and others who hire new teachers. "We had administrators, principals, superintendents, and personnel directors help us determine what beginning teachers need to know," she says. "We were attentive to what they see as everyday needs."

The test includes items on subject-area knowledge and pedagogical knowledge. Madigan says that any teacher who passes the test would be ready to teach. "You learn to teach on the job," she says. "If you have solid subject-area knowledge and professional teaching knowledge under your belt, you're ready to start learning your craft."

FINDING THE RIGHT FIT

Still, some educators caution that such knowledge, while necessary for beginning teachers, is not sufficient and that principals need to look at additional factors before deciding whether to hire a new teacher. "A principal needs to take into consideration the culture of the school and the population of students," says Michael Allen, a program director at the Education Commission of the States. "A teacher who would work well in suburban schools may not do well in inner-city schools or schools with high minority populations. A principal would have to take into consideration whether this teacher is someone who has the skills and personality to handle the kids in their school."

Others point out that principals also want to know whether teachers can work in teams with other teachers, and whether they share the belief that all students can learn. And, since new teachers are fresh out of school, principals need to know if they can be authority figures in the classroom. "They are looking at candidates who have the ability to be adults," says Nancy Moir, director of the New Teacher Center at the University of California at Santa Cruz.

Principals can find the answer to such questions when hiring veteran teachers by looking at recommendations from previous employers. But what about new teachers? For them, the interview process is critical.

Martin Haberman, a distinguished professor in the school of education at the University of Wisconsin–Milwaukee, has developed a set of questions that can help principals predict success among urban teachers (see sidebar, p. 38). The method has been used to hire 30,000 teachers in 160 cities each year, Haberman says. Follow-up studies suggest that the teachers hired through the method perform at least as well as other teachers and remain in the profession longer.

Haberman's approach is aimed at eliciting teachers' points of view on a range of qualities—such as persistence, their approach to "at-risk" students, and the distinction between their professional and personal orientation to children—that together help principals determine whether prospective teachers can relate well to children. "How much teachers know is valuable," Haberman says, "but it only matters if you can relate to kids. If just knowing stuff was all that matters, college professors could teach middle school kids."

RETHINKING THE HIRING PROCESS

While approaches like Haberman's might enable principals to make more informed judgments about prospective teachers, many school leaders may not be able to conduct such thorough inquiries into candidates' backgrounds and approaches to teaching. In a survey of teachers in four states, Edward Liu at the Harvard Graduate School of Education found that, while 80 percent of new teachers interview with the principal, fewer than half interview with other teachers, and only 9 percent interview with parents.

Moreover, Liu's survey found that few schools offer teachers the opportunity to demonstrate their knowledge and skills: only 7.5 percent of the teachers in the four states teach a sample lesson as part of the hiring process. However, the survey also notes that in one state, Michigan, an unusually high number of new teachers—29 percent—had done student teaching at the school where they ended up working. Significantly, new teachers in Michigan reported a relatively high degree of fit between their backgrounds and the schools where they worked.

The study confirms that giving schools the authority to hire teachers is not enough to ensure that the hiring process works well, Liu says. "There's a fair amount of school-based activity, but that didn't necessarily reflect new ways of hiring or richer exchanges of information."

In many cases, principals may not be able to take advantage of the hiring power they have because they hire teachers

DIMENSIONS OF EFFECTIVE TEACHING

Martin Haberman, a distinguished professor in the school of education at the University of Wisconsin–Milwaukee, has developed an interview protocol intended to help principals identify teachers who will be effective in urban schools. The protocol is designed to elicit prospective teachers' attitudes and behaviors and compare them with the attributes of "star" teachers, gleaned from interviews Haberman and his colleagues have conducted. In the interviews, principals examine the following dimensions of teaching and rate prospective teachers as "average," "high," and "star."

1. *Persistence.* Star teachers take as their responsibility the learning of every student, and do not give up until they find better ways of reaching every child.
2. *Protecting learners and learning.* Star teachers do whatever they can to engage students in learning, even if it means violating school policy or standard practice.
3. *Application of generalizations.* Star teachers take principles and concepts from a variety of sources and use them to improve their own practice. They also can see better

too late to be selective. According to the survey, 62 percent of teachers in the four states are hired within 30 days of the start of their teaching responsibilities, and 33 percent are hired after the school year has already started.

Moir, of the New Teacher Center in Santa Cruz, says late hiring does not necessarily result in the selection of poor teachers. "I know in urban settings many principals hire at the last minute," she says. "Folks who hire underprepared than other teachers the connections between students' day-to-day activities and the long-range learning goals they want their students to achieve.

4. *Approach to "at-risk" students.* Star teachers believe that, regardless of the social conditions students face, schools and teachers bear the responsibility to improve their educational opportunities.

5. *Professional versus personal orientation to students.* Star teachers hold strong feelings for their students, but they do not regard a love for them as a prerequisite for their academic success.

6. *Burnout, its causes and cures.* Star teachers use support networks to help them withstand the inevitable pressures they face from large, bureaucratic school systems.

7. *Fallibility.* Star teachers acknowledge that they make mistakes, including serious ones involving human relations.

For Further Information

Haberman Educational Foundation, 4018 Martinshire Dr., Houston, TX 77025-3918. www.altcert.org

teachers say there aren't good candidates. I'm not sure there aren't good candidates."

But Jessica Levin, chief knowledge officer of the New Teacher Project, a Washington, D.C.–based organization, says late hiring does reduce the quality of the pool of teacher applicants. Many well-qualified applicants take jobs in other districts because they cannot wait for the urban schools to hire them, she says. "Many urban districts are receiving a large number of high-quality applicants," Levin says, "but because of the overall hiring process they wait too long to hire, and they lose the best applicants to other districts."

In a recent report, the New Teacher Project identified three systemic factors that contribute to late hiring. First, many districts allow teachers to notify schools that they are leaving as late as August, which makes it difficult for schools to anticipate vacancies. Second, union contracts in many districts grant veteran teachers the first right to vacant positions. Third, budget uncertainties make it difficult to know whether vacant positions can be filled.

The report recommends that districts require earlier vacancy notices, transfer requests, and budget allocations to allow schools to hire teachers earlier in the year. It also highlights several districts, such as Clark County, Nev., San Diego, and Rochester, N.Y., that have implemented at least some of these policies.

Other districts, such as Boston, have addressed some aspects of teacher hiring in collective bargaining agreements. Under a 2000 contract, the district and the teacher union agreed to prohibit tenured teachers from "bumping" first-year teachers from their jobs, curbing a practice that often resulted in late vacancy notices and hiring. However, this limited reform was less than the district had sought and was resisted by the union, which had wanted to retain rights for veteran teachers.

A TWO-WAY STREET

Principals who want to make the right hire should also recognize that the information they *give* to prospective teachers—about their own expectations, about the school, and so forth—may be as important as what they learn about teachers, according to Edward Liu of Harvard. Hiring is often a one-way flow of information, from the prospective teacher to the principal who is doing the hiring, but teachers who really understand the school they are stepping into will be more likely to feel comfortable and stay.

In the end, keeping good teachers in their jobs may be more important than attracting them there in the first place. A study by Richard M. Ingersoll of the University of Pennsylvania found that staffing difficulties schools face stem from the high rate of teacher turnover—some 29 percent of teachers leave teaching in the first three years, he found—rather than from increased student enrollments or retirements. "All the recruitment in the world isn't going to help us retain teachers," says Moir of the New Teacher Center. "They are not going to stay if they don't have high-quality support."

This chapter originally appeared in the January/February 2004 issue of the Harvard Education Letter.

FOR FURTHER INFORMATION

M. Allen. *Eight Questions on Teacher Preparation: What Does the Research Say?* Denver: Education Commission of the States, 2003. Available online at www.ecs.org/html/educationIssues/teachingquality/tpreport/home/summary.pdf

American Board for Certification of Teacher Excellence, 1225 19th St., NW, Suite 400, Washington, DC, 20036; tel: 202-261-2620. www.abcte.org

M. Haberman. "Selecting 'Star' Teachers for Children and Youth in Urban Poverty." *Phi Delta Kappan* 76, no. 10 (June 1995): 777–781.

R.M. Ingersoll. *Is There Really a Teacher Shortage?* Seattle: University of Washington, Center for the Study of Teaching and Policy, September

2003. Available online at http://depts.washington.edu/ctpmail/PDFs/Shortage-RI-09-2003.pdf

J.F. Kain and C. Singleton. "Equality of Educational Opportunity Revisited." *New England Economic Review* (May/June 1996): 109.

J. Levin and M. Quinn. *Missed Opportunities: How We Keep High-Quality Teachers Out of Urban Classrooms*. New York: New Teacher Project, 2003. Available online at www.newteacherproject.org/report.html

E. Liu. "New Teachers' Experience of Hiring: Preliminary Findings from a Four-State Study." Paper prepared for the annual meeting of the American Educational Research Association, Chicago, April 2003. Also see website of the Project on the Next Generation of Teachers, Harvard Graduate School of Education. www.gse.harvard.edu/~ngt

J.K. Rice. *Teacher Quality: Understanding the Effectiveness of Teacher Attributes*. Washington, DC: Economic Policy Institute, 2003. Executive summary is available online at www.epinet.org/content.cfm/books_teacher_quality_execsum_intro

W.L. Sanders and J.C. Rivers. *Cumulative and Residual Effects of Teachers on Future Student Academic Achievement*. Knoxville: University of Tennessee, 1996.

CHAPTER 5

Nontraditional Paths to Teaching

When hiring from alternative-certification programs, proceed with caution

By Debra Viadero

Ask David Wells what he thinks of the teachers who have come to his schools through nontraditional teaching routes, and the Round Rock, Texas, principal offers high praise. Wells has hired a number of teachers from a regional alternative-certification program that supports his school district. He talks about the teachers' ready-made understanding of workplace demands, the life experience they bring to the classroom, and the commitment they demonstrate to their new careers.

"I would say they are more prepared for teaching and they're more prepared for work than the traditional teachers who come right out of undergraduate programs," says Wells, currently the principal of Double File Trail Elementary School.

Jed Lippard, the upper-school director for a public charter school in Cambridge, Mass., has a qualitatively different experience to relate. Lippard recently experimented with hiring a teacher who came to the profession through a state-sponsored program for mid-career entrants. The teacher struggled in the classroom, despite the school's best efforts to mentor him, and left before the school year ended. "Just to assume that good will leads to good teaching is, I think, a tremendous oversimplification," Lippard says. "Being trained as a teacher gives people an extra confirmation that they are suited to the profession or, more importantly, it may give them an indication whether they are not."

Alternative certification programs are churning out new teachers faster than ever, according to the National Center for Alternative Certification (NCAC), a federally funded information clearinghouse. In Wells's home state, for instance, these nontraditional teachers now account for a quarter of the teaching force, according to C. Emily Feistritzer, president of the National Center for Education Information, which directs the NCAC. While most such programs vary, what they offer in common is a quicker path to becoming a teacher and one that does not necessarily require would-be educators to enroll full-time in a college or university.

Some of the push for such programs is coming because policymakers and educators see them as a way to stem potential teacher shortages in the classroom and to create "highly qualified" teachers that meet the requirements of the federal No Child Left Behind Act. Under President Bush, the U.S. Department of Education has also been a strong backer of nontraditional teaching routes, underwriting new studies on the subject, grants to help states set up and expand their alternate-route programs, and Feistritzer's center. President Bush's proposed budget for the 2005 fiscal year set aside $45.3 million for its Transition-to-Teaching grant program, which is aimed at helping states and districts recruit and retain highly qualified mid-career professionals and recent college graduates to teach in schools that are hard pressed for teachers.

Yet the question remains: Are alternative-certification programs an effective way to improve the quality of the nation's teaching force? Or are they a risky gamble for school principals to make? Though nontraditional teaching pathways have been around for nearly 20 years, experts still don't know for sure. Few studies have taken a hard look at the teachers produced by nontraditional preparation programs, and fewer still have examined their potential for diversifying, expanding, and developing the nation's teaching force.

MANY PATHWAYS, MIXED RESULTS

The lack of solid information about this fast-growing segment of educators comes in part because the programs that prepare them are so varied themselves. Forty-three states and the District of Columbia permit teachers to enter the profession without graduating from an approved, university-based teacher-education program. Experts estimate that as many as 600 such programs exist, run variously by school districts, states, universities, private organizations, or some combination thereof.

In some states, such as Massachusetts, Texas, and Georgia, would-be teachers can step into the field just by passing some teaching tests, although this path may not be widely publicized or encouraged. Others, such as Utah, South Carolina, and South Dakota, require teacher candidates to undergo extensive training programs lasting up to three years—almost as long as it takes to complete a traditional undergraduate teacher-education program. Programs also vary in terms of selectivity, the degree to which they offer on-the-job training, the amount of coursework they require, and whom they target. One program, for instance, might set its sights on mid-career professionals from other fields, while another might zero in on classroom aides who already work in schools.

"People tend to treat alternative certification in a generic sense when, in fact, there are at least 50 different systems out there," says Dan Goldhaber, research associate and professor at the University of Washington in Seattle who has studied teacher-quality issues.

Nonetheless, some credible research suggests that at least some of these programs offer some promise in producing effective teachers. The best-known example of that work is a study published in 2004 of Teach For America (TFA), a nationally known Peace Corps–style program that recruits young liberal arts graduates to teach for two years in rural and inner-city schools. The participants, chosen from some of the nation's most selective schools and colleges, attend a five-week summer institute where they take six intensive education courses and attend other workshops and seminars. They also spend several weeks getting their feet wet by teaching summer school. The young recruits step into their regular academic-year classrooms in August or September, but they continue to get support in that first year on the job from their school districts and the national organization.

For the 2004 study, the Washington, D.C.–based research group Mathematica Policy Research, Inc., studied 2,000 students in 17 schools in Baltimore, Houston, Los Angeles, the Mississippi Delta, and New Orleans. In each school, students were randomly assigned either to Teach For America teachers or to educators hired through more typical channels. By the end of the school year, the researchers found, students of the teaching corps' recruits had made larger learning gains on mathematics tests than did children in other classrooms in the same grades and the same schools.

Some critics note, however, that the results don't reveal much about the merits of Teach For America as compared to traditional teacher-education programs. In keeping with its mission, the 14-year-old New York City–based program sends its teachers to some of the poorest and lowest-achieving schools in the nation—places where principals often have to rely on long-term substitutes, emergency hires, and other kinds of alternatively trained teachers just to ensure that there's an adult in every classroom. As a result, the majority of the non-Teach For America teachers in the study were not themselves traditionally certified.

In fact, after two years on the job, the pool of program recruits didn't look much different from the rest of the beginning teachers in the same schools in terms of their education training. One quarter of the Teach For America recruits had earned degrees in education, for instance, compared with 33 percent of the non-TFA novices.

In any case, the results of the Mathematica study may not extend to other programs. "It's fair to say Teach For America doesn't tell you much about alternative teacher-preparation programs in general," says Paul Decker, the researcher who led that study, "because most programs out there don't emulate Teach For America."

To get a better handle on the rest of the programs, Decker is leading another national study, using methodology similar to the Teach For America evaluation, to compare a variety of alternative-preparation programs and gauge their effects on student learning. But that study is just getting under way and results are not expected for another two years.

A TALE OF TWO PROGRAMS

The program that funnels alternatively trained teaching candidates to Wells's school in Round Rock is run by Region XIII, an educational service center for 16 counties in the greater Austin area. It is one of 20 service centers set up by the state in the 1960s to undertake educational activities, such as research or special teacher-training programs, that may be too costly or difficult for individual districts to do on their own. Becky Washington, the senior coordinator of the Region XIII Educator Certification Program, says it accepts about 275 of the 700 to 1,700 candidates who apply each year. Successful applicants must have earned a 2.5 grade-point average in their undergraduate coursework, undergo an interview, submit writing samples, references, and a work history, and pass a basic skills test.

Training typically begins in January, with weekend and evening classes taught at the regional service center. By July of the same year, when the teaching candidates teach summer school for two weeks, they will have accumulated 250 hours of instruction, according to Washington.

In August the novice teachers start work in regular academic-year classrooms, under the supervision of full-time mentors hired by Region XIII. They also continue to attend evening and weekend classes throughout that first year and take state-mandated teaching exams. If they are successful, the teaching candidates can return to their classrooms as full-fledged teachers by the start of the next school year.

Wells says the kind of on-the-job supervision the Region XIII teachers get in their first year of teaching gives them an edge over beginning teachers starting work fresh out of school. Although the latter group may have student-taught in college or graduate school, when they arrive for their first day on the job they leave their mentors behind. "For traditionally certified teachers, that added support base is not there," he says.

The lack of ongoing support was a key issue for the alternatively trained teacher who eventually came to teach in Lippard's charter school. A former lawyer and health-care consultant who asks to remain anonymous, he got a preliminary license to teach through a fast-track program sponsored by the state department of education. The program allows participants to start teaching after passing just two state teaching tests, although it requires them to start taking courses toward full certification within five years. The hiring school district is also expected to provide extensive support to the new teachers in their crucial first year. But when this novice teacher got his first job in a regular public high school outside of Boston, he says, his district never followed through on that expectation.

"You give a stressed, underfunded school system an opportunity to just make a promise and get a new teacher," he says now of that experience, "and they'll promise just about anything."

After a disappointing year, he sought out Prospect Hill Academy, Lippard's small charter school, in the hopes of finding a more supportive environment.

"We hired him knowing he would be a project and thinking the year he'd already had in education would facilitate the transition to a new school," Lippard says. To support his classroom skills, Lippard partnered the new teacher with the school's best math teacher. The headmaster himself also spent two weeks working with the new teacher in the classroom and helping to develop a step-by-step improvement plan. Both the teacher and Lippard agree, however, that the school's efforts proved fruitless. The teacher's classroom-management skills were not improving and he lacked the background knowledge he needed on conducting assessments, understanding children's learning, and communicating with parents. Frustrated and floundering, the teacher left Prospect Hill—and the profession altogether—in the middle of the school year.

Sarah Birkeland, a researcher at Harvard University's Graduate School of Education who has studied 13 "fast-track" alternative teacher-certification programs in districts in California, Connecticut, Louisiana, and Massachusetts, says the support alternatively trained teachers get in that first year on the job is crucial to their sense of success. New teachers lucky enough to land in schools where administrators and educators were willing to mentor them, or where formalized teacher-induction programs were in place, reported having an easier time adjusting to their new careers.

The degree to which a program offered on-the-job support or required teachers to take education courses or pass tests came down in part to differences in the program creators' basic philosophies. "Some thought good teachers were born and you have to find them," Birkeland says, "and some thought they were made." In the former case, programs focused more on selection than on coursework or on-the-job mentoring. In the latter case, the programs devoted more attention to training and postplacement support. Whatever the underlying philosophy, Birkeland says, neither kind of program served a strong gatekeeping function for the profession.

NONTRADITIONAL PREPARATION FOR NONTRADITIONAL SCHOOLS

Lippard has had more success with teacher candidates from New Teachers Collaborative, a year-long program that prepares participants to teach in nontraditional secondary schools. According to Lippard, the program is operated by five regular public or charter schools in Massachusetts and New Hampshire that share elements of the Coalition of Essential Schools teaching philosophy developed by the coalition's founder and chair emeritus Ted Sizer. Paid $15,000 a year to take part, the teaching candidates in the program spend nine of every ten working days in the classroom and attend seminars taught by Sizer and other scholars and practitioners on the tenth. Over the summer, they continue to take seminars on topics ranging from classroom management to discipline-specific teaching methods. The teaching candidates are also assigned mentors. Participants are required to keep weekly journals and produce portfolios that demonstrate their competence.

In this case, Lippard feels that the alternative program is not merely as good as a traditional program, but actually more effective. Not only does it blend academic coursework with real teaching experience, he says, it also prepares teachers specifically for the tasks of teaching in a small, nontraditional school like his. The seminars, for instance, are structured to mimic the collaborative working atmospheres of small schools, and students are required to participate in faculty meetings as part of their year-long induction.

"The reality is that traditional models of teacher preparation are inadequately preparing teachers for the reality of teaching in small schools," Lippard says. "In our schools they are expected to be advisors, to sit on school-improvement committees, or to collaborate with each other on curriculum."

A MIRROR OF THE LABOR MARKET

Alternative certification has often been touted as a way to strengthen the teaching profession by attracting candidates whom traditional teacher-education programs would not reach. But some recent research is challenging commonly held assumptions about this pool of potential teachers.

"It's pretty common for folks to think alternative certification can bring more males and minorities into the profession," says Daniel Humphrey, associate director of SRI International's Center for Education Policy in Menlo Park, Calif. "And that isn't really true."

Humphrey is principal investigator on a three-year national study evaluating the success of seven alternative-preparation routes, including Teach For America and Texas's Region XIII program. The study, which is scheduled to be published this year, has found that more often than not, the nontraditional teachers simply mirror the labor market that surrounds the schools where they teach.

"Most of these teachers end up working in urban districts and they are no more diverse than the traditionally trained teachers who go into the same schools," he says.

He says the SRI researchers were also surprised to find that half of the teachers in the recruit pool they studied had some sort of teaching experience under their belts before they signed up with their programs.

Philip Clayton, for instance, was working as a paraprofessional at Ridgeview Middle School in Round Rock when he was asked to step in for a seventh- and eighth-grade science teacher who had suddenly departed.

"I was 22 and the kids were really drawn to me because of that," he says. When a special education teaching position opened up on the staff the next semester, school administrators agreed to allow Clayton to take it—provided that he go through Region XIII's training program. Clayton, who is now 25, says his early classroom experience helped ease his learning curve. Humphrey says the abundance of teaching experience these teachers have calls into question one of the most popular assumptions critics make about atypical teacher-preparation routes: that they unleash an army of completely inexperienced teachers on schools.

Humphrey has also found, contrary to other commonly held expectations, that only a small percentage of these new recruits fit the stereotypic profile of the highly trained professional looking to give back to society. Fewer than 1 percent of the nontraditional teachers SRI studied were lawyers, for example. Nor did they bring scarce content-area skills to the classroom: Fewer than 10 percent had come out of the math or science professions. "The majority of participants *gained* salary by going into the program," he says. "These are not rocket scientists by any means."

The SRI study offers few statistics, though, on one last area of controversy: whether alternatively certified teachers stay in teaching longer than their counterparts arriving fresh from undergraduate education programs. Feistritzer of the National Center for Alternative Certification points to data from California, Texas, and New Jersey, the states with the longest track record in alternative teacher certification, that suggest that 85 percent of alternatively certified teachers remain in teaching five years after they started—a much higher percentage than for traditionally prepared teachers. But other researchers say they have yet to see convincing national data on that question.

Anecdotally, it makes sense that they do, says Wells, who has seen many teachers come and go in his 11 years as a school principal. "They've had an opportunity to work in other walks of life," he says, "and now they've made a conscious career choice."

FOR FURTHER INFORMATION

Mathematica Policy Research, Inc., P.O. Box 2393, Princeton, NJ 08543-2393; tel: 609-799-3535. www.mathematica-mpr.com/education/

National Center for Alternative Certification, 1901 Pennsylvania Avenue NW, Suite 201, Washington, DC 20006; tel: 866-778-2784. www.teach-now.org

SRI International Alternative Certification Study, 333 Ravenswood Ave., Menlo Park, CA 94025-3493; tel: 650-859-2000. www.sri.com/policy/cep/teachers/altcert.html

Teach For America, 315 West 36th St., 6th Floor, New York, NY 10018; tel: 800-832-1230. www.teachforamerica.org

CHAPTER 6

Taking Care of Novice Teachers

Researchers suggest how to retain new teachers and maintain a first-rate faculty

By Reino Makkonen

sther entered teaching after a long career as an engineer. Her vast scientific knowledge and professional experience made her a unique asset in the low-income, racially diverse urban vocational high school where she taught.

But Esther found the working conditions intolerable. In her view, student discipline was nonexistent throughout the building. Teachers fought among themselves and openly mocked the principal, who never observed them in their classrooms or provided any form of curricular or instructional leadership. Esther found the school disorderly and unsupportive of good teaching, and she left after only one year. She moved to a suburban school near her home that had strong administrators, supportive colleagues, and an orderly, respectful environment. Looking back at her first job, Esther says, "Maybe if I were a better teacher, more experienced . . . maybe I could [have succeeded there]."

But did the responsibility *really* lie with Esther? Are inexperienced teachers—regardless of their talents and subject-area expertise—simply not "good" enough to succeed in urban schools? Or is there something more to be learned from Esther and the thousands of people like her, new teachers who leave their first schools after only a year or two?

Several recent studies have drawn new attention to the problem of novice teacher turnover. Esther was one of 50 new teachers interviewed as part of a multiyear Harvard Graduate School of Education study. Researchers from the school's Project on the Next Generation of Teachers spoke with novice Massachusetts teachers in 1999, then followed up with them in ensuing years to evaluate the teachers' reasons for staying in their schools, moving to new schools, or leaving teaching altogether. As of June 2003, four years after accepting their first positions, well over half were no longer in the schools where they'd started their careers: 16 had moved to new schools and 17 had left public school teaching altogether.

Do these people see their first teaching jobs as stepping-stones to work in other schools or other fields? The evidence suggests the contrary. According to a 2000 Public Agenda study, new teachers actually feel *more* fulfilled and satisfied than college graduates of the same age working in other jobs. But across the country, one out of five leaves the classroom altogether within three years, and almost 40 percent leave within five years. So what happens? How does enthusiasm turn to disillusionment so soon?

Despite the common scapegoat—low salaries—researchers from the Harvard project say that most teachers leave for other reasons. "When people enter teaching, they typically know what the salaries are," explains project co-investigator Sarah Birkeland. "But I think many people are surprised by the poor working conditions in our public schools, particularly mid-career entrants to teaching who have been working in other settings."

STOPPING THE DOWNWARD SPIRAL

As Esther's story illustrates, urban schools are particularly affected by new teacher turnover. According to the National Commission on Teaching and America's Future, in some cities as many as 50 percent of new teachers leave within three years, with many of the most promising educators departing for higher paying suburban districts. Ever greater numbers of less qualified teachers are then left to instruct urban students, many of whom are English-language learners or students from low-income families whose need for highly skilled teachers may, in some ways, be even greater than their peers'.

The result can be a downward spiral that is difficult to interrupt. Research has suggested that the best teachers can improve student achievement by as much as an extra grade level over the course of a year. As outstanding educators leave urban schools, achievement gaps often expand, tensions rise, and working conditions become more dire, leading still more teachers to seek other employment. As Kati Haycock, director of the Washington, D.C.–based Education Trust, pointed out in her 2000 article "No More Settling for Less," many urban schools "are essentially dumping grounds for unqualified teachers, just as they are dumping grounds for the children they serve."

In addition, researchers Eric Hanushek, John Kain, and Steven Rivkin, working with the University of Texas at Dallas' Texas Schools Project, recently found that low student achievement, a problem that plagues urban schools in disproportionate numbers, is strongly associated with high teacher turnover. To most educators, these findings come as no surprise. Though many high-achieving schools in urban districts have been identified through the years, they've long been outnumbered in many cities by their low-performing counterparts—schools that also have trouble keeping the best teachers. But is this problem inevitable? How can today's urban districts stem the flow of effective teachers out of their low-performing schools?

Hanushek, Kain, and Rivkin also looked at the role larger salaries might play in the retention of new teachers in urban settings, and their findings suggest that money—at least in sufficient amounts—may make a difference. According to the Texas study, the average non-minority, female teacher in an urban school would need to be paid 25 percent more than her suburban counterpart to stay on the job. And the required salary differential rises to 40 percent when the teacher has three to five years of experience, the researchers estimate. (The study also found such differentials to be a factor in the retention of male and minority urban teachers but at lower percentages, suggesting that these educators might be more inclined to stay in urban schools despite the lack of a substantial difference in pay.)

However, the authors are quick to note that their salary calculations do not address the important underlying concern of teacher quality. "Any salary adjustments designed to reduce teacher turnover will affect both high-quality teachers and low-quality teachers, tending to increase the retention of both," they explain. "Spending the substantial sums implied by our estimates solely to reduce turnover, without explicitly considering the much more important issue of quality, would make for bad policy."

IMPROVING CONDITIONS

In an era of tight city budgets and limited resources, large-scale pay raises or incentive programs may not even be possible—except in districts lucky enough to secure private funding. Fortunately, several recent studies have suggested that other approaches—those aimed at improving working conditions, particularly for newer teachers who are at the highest risk of leaving the profession—can also be effective.

Mentoring and Instructional Support. Inexperienced teachers learning for the first time about classroom management, curriculum, and district paperwork are commonly overwhelmed by a full load of classes. When researchers from the Public Education Network (PEN, a national association of local education funds and community groups) recently interviewed more than 200 novice instructors about their experiences on the job, the new teachers pointed to mentoring—being paired with experienced instructors—as the most effective form of assistance and support in their first years.

Administrators cannot, however, simply assign a new teacher to a veteran or mentoring team without providing a coherent structure for the partnership. The most successful programs, the PEN survey suggests, regularly schedule common meeting times and partner teachers according to subject-area and grade-level expertise.

Also, the new teachers who participated in the PEN study noted that not all good teachers make good mentors. The most successful ones have good interpersonal skills, knowledge of how the school and district operate, and credibility with administrators.

Structured Discipline Policies. Although problems with student behavior play a role in many new teachers' decisions to leave their jobs, both the Harvard and PEN studies suggest that most educators fault the school structure rather than the students themselves for breakdowns in student discipline. Other teachers cite the importance of having an accessible and supportive principal. New teachers were thankful, and sometimes surprised, when school leaders publicly supported their decisions in discipline matters. Several studies therefore recommend that schools adopt carefully designed discipline codes, rules of behavior, and safety protocols to support teachers, especially novice ones.

"I think [a lot of] new teachers get turned off from teaching because they realize that too much of their time is spent disciplining students," says Jennie Diefendorf, a first-year teacher at Boston's Academy of the Pacific Rim, a public charter school. "Students [at the Academy] are immersed in this discipline code from the first day they enter the building, and there are tangible consequences spelled out for violations of the code."

At the Academy, students must be on time, prepared, and respectful. If they are not, they go home. There are no exceptions. This system is well known and endorsed by students, parents, and teachers throughout the system. And, while such a "zero tolerance" policy might be more difficult to implement at a large, traditionally organized urban school, research suggests that this kind of schoolwide clarification of discipline codes and expectations might help more new teachers stay in the profession.

Differentiated Roles and Career Ladders. Most young college graduates do not believe teachers have good opportunities for advancement and leadership, according to several recent studies. Despite their initial enthusiasm, talented and creative young instructors are often unwilling to remain in a job many view as unchanging. Unlike previous generations of teachers, today's classroom leaders see their peers earning promotions and recognition in such fields as technology and consulting, while they exhaustingly crawl along a uniform salary scale. With a growing variety of other professional options for today's graduates, top teachers may be less likely than their predecessors to stay in one job for their entire career, especially if they see limited opportunities for growth.

In response, researchers recommend that the best teachers be shifted into alternate roles for additional pay, working as staff developers and curriculum coordinators, or conducting grant-funded projects and research at the school. Others suggest a more formal professional career ladder that includes levels such as "intern," "resident," and "master instructor." These reforms would enhance the reputation of the profession and attract high-quality candidates to teaching, experts say (see chapters 2 and 8).

"New teachers may want to focus intently on their teaching for the first several years," Harvard's Birkeland says. "But many also want to know that other challenges are ahead once they begin to feel comfortable in the classroom."

NO "NO-COST" SOLUTIONS

As the research suggests, retaining high-quality teachers may be an even bigger challenge in the coming years than recruiting them, particularly in the low-performing schools that need good teachers the most. Virtually any efforts to improve working conditions for new teachers, even those not directly tied to financial incentives, come with a price tag. It requires human resource reallocation, for example, to allow a veteran teacher to serve as a mentor or to promote an effective teacher up a career ladder to curriculum leader.

Research and experience also suggest, however, that inaction can be costly. School districts annually spend vast amounts of resources to recruit, replace, and retrain staff, and students pay every time a strong teacher leaves a school community and is replaced by a less skilled or less invested educator. Given the alternative of high teacher turnover—especially in urban schools—taking care of new teachers may well be a district's best bargain.

This chapter originally appeared in the May/June 2004 issue of the Harvard Education Letter.

FOR FURTHER INFORMATION

E. Hanushek, J. Kain, and S. Rivkin. "The Revolving Door: A Path-Breaking Study of Teachers in Texas Reveals that Working Conditions Matter More than Salary." *Education Next* 4, no. 1 (Winter 2004): 77–82. Unabridged research article available online at www.educationnext.org/unabridged/20041/76.pdf

K. Haycock. "No More Settling for Less." *Thinking K–16* 4, no. 1 (Spring 2000): 3–12. Available online at www2.edtrust.org/NR/rdonlyres/ E0A47827-6FA9-4BAD-A157-60ABB852F51A/0/k16_spring2000.pdf

S.M. Johnson and Project on the Next Generation of Teachers. *Finders and Keepers: Helping New Teachers Survive and Thrive in Our Schools*. San Francisco: Jossey-Bass, 2004.

H. Lankford, S. Loeb, and J. Wyckoff. "Teacher Sorting and the Plight of Urban Schools: A Descriptive Analysis." *Educational Evaluation and Policy Analysis* 24, no. 1 (Spring 2002): 37–62.

A Sense of Calling: Who Teaches and Why. New York: Public Agenda, 2000. Available online at www.publicagenda.org/specials/teachers/ teachers.htm

Teaching Commission. *Teaching at Risk: A Call to Action*. New York: CUNY Graduate Center, January 14, 2004. Available online at www.thet eachingcommission.org/publications/FINAL_Report.pdf

The Voice of the New Teacher. Washington, DC: Public Education Network, 2003. Available online at www. publiceducation.org/pdf/PEN_Pubs/ Voice_of_the_New_Teacher.pdf

CHAPTER 7

New Teacher Induction

The right system of supports can help new teachers grow into their jobs

By Susan M. Kardos

New teachers often experience a turbulent descent into their first teaching assignment. They must make quick decisions about how to manage their classrooms and maintain order among their students. They must figure out what to teach and which resources to use, how to pace their lessons, and how to engage students with varied abilities and interests. They often find themselves wondering, "How on earth will I teach this tomorrow?"

No matter how well prepared a new teacher might be, beginning a new teaching job can be extraordinarily difficult. Sharon Feiman-Nemser, an expert on mentoring, induction, and new teacher learning, explains that new teachers have two jobs: "They have to teach, and they have to learn to teach" (Feiman-Nemser, 2001). Despite this double challenge, it is surprising how few schools or districts anticipate the needs of new teachers and provide programs to meet them.

Since 1999, the Project on the Next Generation of Teachers at the Harvard Graduate School of Education, directed by Susan Moore Johnson, has been studying issues related to attracting, supporting, and retaining new teachers.[1] Through multiple studies using both quantitative and qualitative methodologies, we have described new teachers' experiences and their need for overt and organized support in their early years of teaching (Johnson & Project on the Next Generation of Teachers, 2004). The ability of schools and districts to support new teachers' development will determine both how well new teachers are teaching and how well they are learning to teach.

Recent research documents what teachers, students, and their parents have long known: having good teachers has an effect on how much students learn. If new teachers are to develop into effective and successful teachers, they will need much more than the kind of "induction" one teacher in our longitudinal study of new Massachusetts teachers described: "Here are your keys, here's your room, good luck." Even in schools where new teachers are warmly welcomed and help is generously offered, formal and deliberate programs need to be in place so that new teachers will not be left alone to figure out how to teach. An induction program can help a new teacher understand how to conduct her first parent meeting or curriculum night, or how to adapt her lessons based on a better understanding of her students' work. By allowing for interaction among teachers with varying levels of experience, induction programs can also alleviate some of the painful professional isolation beginning teachers experience. In addition to easing the transition and increasing the chances that beginning teachers will have early success with their students, good induction programs provide constructive learning opportunities critical to teachers' ongoing development.

Induction programs can also play an important role in reducing teacher turnover, according to recent research conducted by Richard Ingersoll of the University of Pennsylvania and Thomas Smith of Vanderbilt University. Teacher turnover is a critical problem for both student learning and the organizational health of a school. It can be both a cause and an effect of low-performing schools (Ingersoll & Smith, 2004). Students lose out if they are taught by inexperienced teachers year after year. High turnover disrupts the sense of community within a school and can make it hard for teachers and administrators to pursue long-term goals. And the costs for schools and districts can be high if the initial investment in each new hire is lost after a year or two.

MANY SHAPES AND SIZES

In an effort to address these issues, mentoring and induction programs are proliferating across the country. The proportion of new teachers who report that they have participated in some sort of formal induction program increased from approximately 40 percent to 80 percent between 1990 and 2000 (Ingersoll & Smith, 2004). In 2003, 30 states had official statewide induction programs, and 16 states required and funded induction programs (Quality Counts, 2003).

The programs themselves vary considerably: some are school-based, some are district-based, and some are statewide. Some consist mainly of matching a new teacher with a more experienced mentor teacher for formal or informal consultation. Others are more comprehensive systems with multiple, integrated components (seminars, subject-area coaching, grade-level teams), and are grounded in the values of the school.

One school-based program that demonstrates many of the key features of an effective induction system is located at Evanston (Ill.) Township High School (ETHS).[2] Established fully in 2002–03, the new teacher induction program is an integrated system of programs, people, attitudes, and practices that provide for the support and development of beginning teachers.[3] It is designed to last from hiring to award of tenure, and focuses not only on new teachers' daily survival but on their long-term development of teaching expertise.

At ETHS, the hiring process is considered part of a new teacher's induction, and the entire department participates. Candidates visit classes and may be asked to teach a sample lesson. Meanwhile, they begin to learn about professional norms, practices, and expectations through the hiring process.

Before the school year begins, new teachers attend ETHS 101, a four-day course meant to introduce new teachers to the culture of the school, help them develop classroom management strategies, and get them thinking about ways to build relationships with their students. The course also introduces new teachers to the district's work on standards and assessment. New teachers also attend a district orientation and reception—an example of how a school-based program can integrate with district-level initiatives.

New teachers at ETHS are assigned mentors in their subject areas to provide one-on-one practical assistance in planning and teaching— "nuts and bolts ideas about teaching," as one teacher put it—and to provide social and emotional support. Each department also has one or two staff developers, expert teachers who have release time to observe and assist new teachers with their classroom teaching. During a teacher's first year she also participates in the Mentor Program, which consists of twice-monthly inter-departmental seminar meetings facilitated by experienced teachers to discuss topics such as parent conferences, student discipline, closing the achievement gap between minority and nonminority students, and understanding the new teacher evaluation system.

In the second year, teachers take an on-site course called Studying Skillful Teaching, which is taught by administrators and veteran teachers.[4] This is the equivalent of a graduate course, where new teachers study pedagogy in depth. Whereas one new teacher described the Mentor Program seminars as "learning the ropes," Studying Skillful Teaching delves deeper into issues of teaching and learning. One new teacher explained that the course gave her "a different way of thinking about teaching, and it gives you a support group of persons who may be faced with the same situations." The fact that the course is taught by high-level administrators and veteran teachers further reinforces the idea that school leaders and teacher leaders support new teacher induction.

ETHS's professional culture emphasizes the responsibility that experienced teachers in the school share for the beginning teachers. New teachers need not depend on a single relationship or a single experience or session to get the support they need. What new teachers do not get from their staff developer they may find in their work with their mentor. What they do not find in their Mentor Program meetings they may find in their departmental meetings or in collaboration with their colleagues. And what they began to learn in the hiring process is built upon and vastly expanded in ETHS 101 and beyond.

PARTNERSHIP-BASED PROGRAMS

While some induction programs are school-based, others are not. Partnerships with districts, states, and universities can bring needed funding, technical assistance, and human resources to schools, especially to schools that serve low-income students and tend to struggle to secure funds for mentor salaries or to find mentors willing or able to work with new teachers. One example of a statewide program is Connecticut's Beginning Educator Support and Training (BEST) program, which is operated as a partnership between the state of Connecticut and local districts.[5] This two-year comprehensive program for all new classroom teachers is aimed at increasing new teacher retention, fostering reflective practice among new teachers, improving the practice of experienced teachers, and developing teacher leadership.

As its central component, the program uses mentors (or support teams) to assist new teachers, but it also features mandatory collaborative work time with the mentor or other colleagues, ongoing professional development seminars, content-area external networks, and a portfolio assessment. The external network is a statewide listserv of teachers organized by content area. Through the listserv, new teachers get regular information about resources, professional development, and their teaching portfolio.

In their second year, new teachers prepare a teaching portfolio to document their planning, teaching, assessment of student learning, and reflection. The portfolios are assessed by trained evaluators with relevant subject-matter competence. New teachers must have a passing score on their portfolio in order to be eligible for a provisional license. If they do not pass in their second year of teaching, they can resubmit a portfolio in their third year. If they do not pass in their third year, they are unable to continue to teach in Connecticut.

Certain aspects of the program are administered and funded statewide, such as technical assistance provided to districts, mentor training, and portfolio evaluation. Individual districts are responsible for appointing a facilitator for the program, recruiting experienced teachers to serve as mentors, providing their own orientation and support program for new teachers, and securing release time and space (and stipends) for new teachers and their mentors. The program benefits all new teachers, regardless of their preparation. Notably, it is seen as a crucial source of support for the increasing number of alternatively prepared new teachers entering the teaching force (see chapter 5). The director of Connecticut's Alternative Route to Certification's (ARC) program has remarked, "I sleep better at night knowing that the BEST program exists" (Johnson, Birkeland, & Peske, in press).

A more complex partnership is the Santa Cruz New Teacher Project (SCNTP), which provides induction for 30 school districts (700 new teachers) in California and involves the University of California at Santa Cruz, the Santa Cruz County Office of Education, and the 30 participating districts.[6] The program, for first- and second-year teachers, focuses sharply on teacher development and expertise of both novice and veteran teachers. It is based in the classroom and on teacher learning. Novice teachers are matched with highly trained, experienced teachers, hired and released from their districts, who act as mentors. Both the new teachers and the mentors are engaged in ongoing professional development aimed at improving practice and continued growth. The mentor relationship lasts for two years. Mentors meet with new teachers before school begins and continue to meet with them weekly. New teachers participate in content-specific workshops on topics such as working with English-language learners, differentiating instruction, and working with special population students. They also complete a formative assessment, using tools such as classroom profiles, collaborative logs, individual learning plans, self-assessments, observation tools, and protocols for the analysis of student work to help them improve their practice.

LESSONS FROM MODEL PROGRAMS

Much can be learned from these and other model programs.[7] A growing body of research, both qualitative and quantitative, is beginning to clarify which features constitute good induction systems. Richard Ingersoll and Thomas Smith's work, for example, shows that teachers who receive the following kinds of supports are less likely to leave their schools at the end of their first year: a mentor in the same field; common planning time with other teachers in the same subject; regular collaboration with other teachers; and participation in an external network of teachers. The more of these individual supports new teachers have, the less likely they are to leave their school (Ingersoll & Smith, 2004).

More generally, research by the Project on the Next Generation of Teachers concludes that new teacher induction must be coherent and sustained.[8] Induction programs need the full financial support that it takes to run them well and the support of district leaders and principals to assure that time and space is allotted for new teachers to meet with qualified, trained, and compensated mentors—in a way that is flexible enough to respond to new teachers' emerging needs. And, in addition to the full endorsement of the school's administrators and teacher leaders, successful programs require the willing participation of new teachers themselves. They are most effective when embedded in a workplace culture that supports teacher learning and development. Thus, the effectiveness of any given induction program, such as Connecticut's BEST or the Santa Cruz New Teacher Project, may well depend on the context of the school in which it is implemented.

The Next Generation of Teachers researchers also found that effective induction is a *system* of supports, not merely a menu of offerings. It has multiple, interconnected parts, all of which have as their primary focus classroom teaching and student learning. Induction is not meant to simply provide new teachers with social-emotional support or help them navigate a complicated bureaucracy or master administrative and logistical tasks. Central to the work must be the new teacher's curriculum, her pedagogy, and her students. She must have formalized opportunities and common time to seek practical advice from experienced colleagues, to observe model lessons and to be observed, and to translate ideas into specific methods for use in her classroom.

It is important to distinguish comprehensive induction programs from simple mentoring programs. Until fairly recently, most so-called induction programs were simple one-to-one mentoring programs. While mentoring has been found to have a positive impact on new teacher retention (Ingersoll

& Kralik, 2004), the nature and quality of new teachers' experiences in these programs vary widely (Johnson, Kardos, Kauffman, Liu, & Donaldson, 2004; Kardos, 2004). Furthermore, there is a vast distinction between simple one-to-one mentoring programs and comprehensive induction programs, within which mentoring may feature prominently. The underlying premise of one-to-one mentoring is that a "good match" can be made between a master teacher and a beginning teacher. However, teaching styles, philosophies, or personalities are often divergent, and school structures do not support the mentoring relationship with common meeting or classroom observation time, adequate incentives and rewards for mentoring, or effective mentor training. Increasingly cognizant of the limits of one-to-one mentoring, education leaders are beginning to see the need for more comprehensive induction systems.

Finally, our research indicates that it is essential that new teacher induction be integrated into the new teacher's professional life and the professional practice of her school. That is, induction should not be something that she *leaves her school to get*, but a natural, ongoing, and sustained part of her development as a teacher in the context of her school. The farther away from schools these programs are located, the more difficult it is for them to respond to new teachers' specific needs and help new teachers understand their own school's mission, norms, values, curricula, policies, and practices. As much as possible, induction systems should be located at the school site. After all, it is in classrooms and in schools where new teachers succeed or fail with their students and decide whether or not to stay in teaching.

NOTES

1. For more information on the Project on the Next Generation of Teachers, visit www.gse.harvard.edu/~ngt.

2. This summary is drawn from *Finders and Keepers: Helping New Teachers Survive and Thrive in Our Schools,* by Susan Moore Johnson and the Project on the Next Generation of Teachers (2004).

3. Some elements of the ETHS induction program have been in existence for several years, even as far back as 1997. However, the comprehensive induction program, as it currently exists, began in the 2002–03 school year.

4. This is a course on pedagogy adapted from *The Skillful Teacher: Building Your Teaching Skills,* by Jonathan Saphier and Robert Gower (1997).

5. This summary is drawn from the 2004 report issued by the Alliance for Excellent Education entitled "Tapping the Potential: Retaining and Developing High-Quality New Teachers," Appendix A Case Studies.

6. This summary is drawn from the 2004 report issued by the Alliance for Excellent Education entitled "Tapping the Potential," Appendix A Case Studies.

7. The following induction programs were featured in the 2004 report issued by the Alliance for Excellent Education entitled "Tapping the Potential: Retaining and Developing High-Quality New Teachers": Louisiana Framework for Inducting, Retaining, and Supporting Teachers (LaFIRST) and The Toledo Plan. Induction programs also featured in (Susan Moore Johnson & The Project on the Next Generation of Teachers, 2004): Brookline High School, Brookline, Mass.; Murphy Elementary School, Boston, Mass. In their book, *New Teacher Induction,* Annette Breaux and Harry Wong (Breaux & Wong, 2003) provide contact information for 30 induction programs purported to be highly successful and replicable.

8. See also Britton, Raizen, Paine, and Huntley (2000) and Alliance for Excellent Education (2004).

REFERENCES

Alliance for Excellent Education. (2004). *Tapping the potential: Retaining and developing high-quality new teachers*. Washington, DC: Alliance for Excellent Education.

Breaux, A. L., & Wong, H. K. (2003). *New teacher induction: How to train, support, and retain new teachers*. Mountain View, CA: Harry K. Wong.

Britton, E., Raizen, S., Paine, L., & Huntley, M. A. (2000). *More swimming, less sinking: Perspectives on teacher induction in the U.S. and abroad*. Washington, DC: National Commission on Mathematics and Science Teaching for the 21st Century.

Feiman-Nemser, S. (2001). From preparation to practice: Designing a continuum to strengthen and sustain teaching. *Teachers College Record, 103*, 1013–1055.

Ingersoll, R., & Kralik, J. M. (2004). *The impact of mentoring on teacher retention: What the research says*. Denver: Education Commission of the States.

Ingersoll, R., & Smith, T. (2004). Do teacher induction and mentoring matter? *NASSP Bulletin, 87*(638), 28–40.

Johnson, S. M., Birkeland, S. E., Peske, H. G. (in press). Life in the "fast track": How states seek to balance incentives and quality in alternative teacher certification programs. In *Politics of Education Administration yearbook*. Thousand Oaks, CA: Corwin Press.

Johnson, S. M., Kardos, S. M., Kauffman, D., Liu, E., & Donaldson, M. L. (2004). The support gap: New teachers' experiences in high-income and low-income schools. *Education Policy Analysis Archives, 12*(61).

Johnson, S. M., & Project on the Next Generation of Teachers. (2004). *Finders and keepers: Helping new teachers survive and thrive in our schools*. San Francisco: Jossey-Bass.

Kardos, S. M. (2004). *Supporting and sustaining new teachers in schools: The importance of professional culture and mentoring.*, Cambridge, MA: Harvard University.

Quality Counts. (2003). *The teacher gap*. Bethesda, MD: Author.

Saphier, J., & Gower, R. R. (1997). *The skillful teacher: Building your teaching skills*. Carlisle, MA: Research for Better Teaching.

CHAPTER 8

Building a Better Career Ladder

A new spin on old reforms may help keep today's teachers in the classroom

By Morgaen L. Donaldson

Only a few years ago, Austin Clark was a promising, committed young math teacher at North Carolina's Easton High School. Although he enjoyed discussing calculus, posing algebra puzzles, and debating Tar Heel basketball prospects with his students, he yearned for something more from his work as a teacher. Soon he began to seek out opportunities to lead workshops on the use of technology in instruction at the state, regional, and even national level. However, he deliberately kept a low profile within his own school, where he feared his relative inexperience would prompt his fellow teachers to discount his perspective.

As he moved into leadership roles outside his school, however, Austin found himself pulled in different directions. "I had several options in the profession," he recalls, "but all of them took me out of the classroom." Five years after beginning his teaching career, Austin left teaching to pursue his doctorate, making the difficult decision "to say goodbye to not just the hundreds of students that I taught but the thousands of students that I would teach."

Looking back, Austin reflects, "It would have been enticing to be able to reach a certain point in the profession and have the profession recognize my other contributions and allow me to pursue them, instead of treating them as 'add-ons' or 'extras.'"

Austin's story resembles those of many of his contemporaries. As research by the Project on the Next Generation of Teachers (PNGT) demonstrates, new teachers today, no matter how committed to the classroom, also expect their careers to offer them a variety of opportunities over time. Traditionally, the teaching career has been flat and undifferentiated, a structure that has seemed to suit most teachers. In 1975, Dan Lortie, a leading scholar on teachers and their work, observed, "Teachers continue to oppose internal differentiation in rewards on grounds other than seniority or education; their behavior has been consistently egalitarian" (1975, p. 102). Today's teachers, however, seem to differ markedly from the earlier generation. Yet if the attitudes and expectations of teachers have changed in the past 30 years, has the teaching profession kept pace? Does teaching provide today's teachers with what they need to remain in the profession?

NEW ROLES AND RESPONSIBILITIES

Practitioners and researchers agree that the teacher work force is currently undergoing a shift. Veterans who started teaching in the 1960s and 1970s and spent the duration of their careers in the classroom are retiring in droves. Relatively new teachers, like Austin, will soon predominate in the work force. Career ladders that offer new roles and expanded authority may be an effective way to retain and sustain this new group of teachers.

Broadly defined, a career ladder rewards teachers with graduated pay and recognition based on merit, often assessed on the basis of classroom performance or service to the school. In some cases a teacher may receive credit for essentially expanding her classroom responsibilities—for instance, tutoring after school. But this kind of ladder doesn't offer the variety of responsibilities that new teachers say they are looking for. The career ladders discussed in this article are those that offer teachers differentiated roles along with pay and recognition. Such roles might include math coach, mentor, grade-level team director, or curriculum coordinator.

Experimentation with new roles and expanded authority for teachers began in the 1980s, when many states and districts instituted career ladders. Despite this promising start, these initial efforts were largely abandoned in the early 1990s due to mixed results and budget cuts. Today career ladders are beginning to surface once again. With the implementation of various large-scale reform initiatives and the entry of a new generation of teachers, career ladders may be more likely to succeed than they were only a few decades ago.

THE WAVE OF THE PAST

In 1986, the Carnegie Forum on Education and the Economy recommended that districts "restructure the teaching force and introduce a new category of Lead Teachers" in part to "make teachers' salaries and career opportunities competitive with those in other professions" (1986, pp. 55–56). Fearing an impending teacher shortage and persuaded that a restructuring of their work would retain and motivate teachers, about half of the states in the country and many local districts heeded the Forum's call and hastily enacted career ladder programs by the early 1990s.

Once engaged in planning and implementation, however, teachers and district leaders realized that this reform was more problematic than anticipated. First, it challenged the egalitarianism held dear by teachers. As a result, most career ladders wound up with only three rungs, based on widely acknowledged differences in levels of classroom experience: student teacher, provisional (pre-tenured) teacher, and tenured teacher. Although these rungs were given different labels, the relatively flat career trajectory of the profession remained unaltered and teachers' roles remained undifferentiated from one level to the next.

Second, teachers became skeptical when they saw less qualified colleagues moving up the ladders. In Tennessee, Susan Rosenholtz (1987) found that teachers watched the career ladder evaluation process carefully. When mediocre colleagues received promotions, they deemed the process illegitimate and avoided participation.

Third, career ladders required considerable financial support, which was subject to the ebbs and flows of political support. In the early 1990s, many districts reallocated funds toward student assessment and away from teacher career development. In some cases, the defeat of a career ladder proponent in the state legislature or governor's office hastened the decline of career ladder funding.

Due to these obstacles, few of the career ladders instituted in the 1980s and early 1990s introduced graduated roles and differentiated responsibilities into teachers' work. Predictably, the research on these career reforms is inconclusive. Some researchers found that the presence of a career ladder increased the satisfaction and retention of participating teachers (Conley & Levinson, 1993). Others found career ladders created acrimony, distrust, and stress among faculty (Henson & Hall, 1993). Sometimes, schools and teachers within the same district experienced the creation of career ladders quite differently (Hart, 1994). Two of the biggest issues affecting career ladder success were the faculty's capacity to trust that administrators would evaluate them fairly and teachers' willingness to accept differentiation within their ranks.

CHANGES IN ATTITUDE

Although many states and districts abandoned such reforms in the early 1990s, there is growing evidence that a new round of career ladder implementation is now underway. Critics ask how these reforms will differ from the rather unsteady experiments of the 1980s. For several reasons, today's career ladder initiatives are more promising than those of the past.

First, new teachers are entering the work force with new attitudes about their careers. In a study of 50 new Massachusetts teachers, PNGT researchers found that although 26 wanted to spend their entire career in schools, only 10 of these teachers planned to remain exclusively in the classroom (Johnson & Project on the Next Generation of Teachers, 2004). Most of the others wanted to take on additional roles, such as literacy specialist or lead teacher. Moreover, there is some evidence that these teachers eschew the traditional career path from classroom teacher to principal. One new teacher in this study spoke for many in saying she would "definitely not" enter administration—"too many hours, not enough money, not worth all the headaches" (p. 231). There is also evidence that these teachers are less averse to differentiation within their ranks. Helena (Mont.) high school teacher Geoff Proctor, for instance, says, "I would love to see us grant some evaluative duties to people within our department who have a much better idea of what we do than our administrators."

Second, standards-based reform—which has swept the nation's schools in recent years—has generated changes in curriculum and instruction that create leadership opportunities for teachers. Richard Barnes, former teacher, superintendent, and dean of the University of Southern Maine's College of Education and Human Development, says that new demands for accountability "mean that skilled teachers need to be available for real-time coaching and support for colleagues … [and] because of this, there has been a rise of the lead teacher and literacy or math coach role." Teachers have led literacy task forces, data assessment teams, and collaborative efforts to design better instruction. Sidestepping the head-on confrontation with teacher egalitarianism that occurred in the 1980s, today's focus on student performance has wrought a quiet, steady restructuring of the teacher profession.

Many teachers find these new roles rewarding. Karen Mac-Donald says her role as a "teaching strategist" in an elementary school in Portland, Maine, allowed her "to observe other classrooms and learn from my colleagues … about curriculum, assessment, and instructional strategies." Having exited this role after five years, Karen returned to the classroom "so that I can use what I have learned."

Efforts to standardize curriculum and testing may also reduce many teachers' opposition to career restructuring by introducing more objectivity into evaluation. Richard Barnes observes that "there is much more likely to be a shared agreement or consensus today [than in the 1980s] between teachers and administrators about what constitutes effective teaching, and therefore teachers who are awarded extra status or compensation for career accomplishments are more likely to be supported by their colleagues as deserving of the honor." Moreover, value-added assessment may allow schools to isolate the impact of individual teachers on student learning. While this method of assessment is still imperfect, it may provide a more objective basis for evaluation and promotion. Following the lead of Tennessee and other states, Pennsylvania has mandated that all its schools use this method of assessment by 2005–06, although teachers' rewards or penalties are not currently contingent on these assessments.

Finally, as districts have grown increasingly concerned about new teacher retention, a growing number have launched mentoring and induction programs that offer new roles for experienced teachers (see chapter 7). Nationally, participation in induction programs has doubled in the last decade (Smith & Ingersoll, in press). One recent study found that mentoring and induction programs may promote "a larger continuum of teacher development" through new roles and responsibilities for experienced teachers (Katz & Feiman-Nemser, 2004, p. 115). Within these programs, teachers have acted as coordinators or mentors, taught courses on topics such as classroom management and instructional differentiation, and engaged in sustained dialogue with novices about teaching and learning.

THE ROCHESTER MODEL

The Career in Teaching (CIT) program in the Rochester, N.Y., public schools is an example of a career ladder program that offers differentiated roles to participants. The program, which was one of the few to weather the cutbacks of the early 1990s, consists of four rungs: intern, resident, professional, and lead teacher. Pre-tenured teachers—a group that most districts treat as an undifferentiated whole—are divided into interns and resident teachers. Interns, or novice teachers, are mentored by lead teachers. When an intern's lead teacher judges that she is sufficiently prepared to become a resident teacher, the intern moves into this category. "Most teachers learn their pedagogical habits and classroom management habits during the first year or two of teaching," comments Adam Urbanski, president of the Rochester Teachers Association. With proper mentoring from senior teachers "they don't have to learn by trial and error," he says. "And they don't get as quickly frustrated as they would if they had no support."

As residents, Rochester teachers are required to obtain a master's degree within five years. Their tuition is reimbursed through the program. "They view the reimbursement for tuition as an investment that the system makes in them," Urbanski explains. "It is a way of valuing them."

Further differentiation appears at the upper rungs. When an intern becomes a professional teacher, she takes on new authority. Professional teachers may evaluate their peers in the Performance Appraisal Review for Teachers (PART). They may also participate in the governance of the CIT program. Six teachers and an equal number of administrators sit on the Joint Governing Panel, which oversees lead teacher selection, evaluates mentors and lead teachers, and reviews all appeals regarding the CIT program. The panel also makes employment recommendations to the school board, via the superintendent and union president. As of 2002, almost all of these recommendations had been enacted.

Lead teachers, who occupy the top rung of the CIT ladder, have several distinct responsibilities. Like professional teachers, they may evaluate their peers and sit on the CIT panel. In addition, they serve as mentors for new teachers and veteran teachers who need support or, in especially serious cases, intervention. Lead teachers are selected on the basis of outstanding ability to teach and work with colleagues. These experts remain in the classroom part-time, but are released from 20 to 50 percent of their teaching duties (with compensation) to perform mentoring and other leadership tasks. Importantly, lead teachers evaluate their mentees, whether novice or struggling veteran, an assessment that factors heavily in the district's employment decisions. Thus, along with extra pay and recognition, this role offers important new responsibilities to those who hold it.

By placing evaluation and career ladder decisions largely in the hands of well-regarded teachers, the CIT program has managed to avoid the accusations of unfair evaluation that stymied early career ladder efforts. A well-articulated appeals process has undoubtedly contributed to CIT's success in this regard. The longevity of the program is one indicator of its success; another is its impact on teacher retention.

"The teachers give an overwhelming response to this program," Urbanski notes. "The mentoring program has substantially increased our retention rates, which were around 65 percent when we first started about 18 years ago and are now around 92 percent." This number is unusually high, especially for an urban district.

Despite the success of the CIT program and others around the country, career ladders may still be hampered by the considerable financial support they require from districts. When compared to a flat, undifferentiated teacher career structure, career ladders require more money and, as with all reform, this money is not guaranteed. Florida's state legislature, for example, has passed legislation authorizing career ladders but, to date, has failed to fund the initiative. Still, over the long run, these programs may save money if, like Rochester's, they are able to reduce turnover among experienced teachers. And, in fact, given the changes in new teachers' attitudes and expectations, school districts may not have a choice. To retain skilled teachers like Austin, a career ladder may not only be smart, it may be essential.

REFERENCES

Carnegie Forum on Education and the Economy. (1986). *A nation prepared: Teachers for the 21st century*. New York: Carnegie Forum on Education and the Economy.

Conley, S., & Levinson, R. (1993). Teacher work redesign and job satisfaction. *Educational Administration Quarterly, 29*, 453–478.

Hart, A. W. (1994). Creating teacher leadership roles. *Educational Administration Quarterly, 30*, 472–497.

Henson, B. E., & Hall, P. M. (1993). Linking performance evaluation and career ladder programs: Reactions of teachers and principals in one district. *Elementary School Journal, 93*, 323–353.

Johnson, S. M., & Project on the Next Generation of Teachers. (2004). *Finders and keepers: Helping new teachers survive and thrive in our schools*. San Francisco: Jossey-Bass.

Katz, D., & Feiman-Nemser, S. (2004). New teacher induction in a culture of professional development. In J. I. Goodlad & T. J. Mackinnon (Eds.), *The teaching career* (pp. 96–116). New York: Teachers College Press.

Lortie, D. C. (1975). *Schoolteacher: A sociological study*. Chicago: University of Chicago Press.

Rosenholtz, S. J. (1987). Education reform strategies: Will they increase teacher commitment? *American Journal of Education, 95*, 534–562.

Smith, T., & Ingersoll, R. (in press). Reducing teacher turnover: What are the components of effective induction? *American Educational Research Journal, 41*(2).

CHAPTER 9

Putting National Board Certification to the Test

This credential for veteran teachers is drawing high praise—and tough questions, too

By David T. Gordon

n February 1997, David Lustick was itching for a challenge. He had earned a master's degree in education and taught high school chemistry in New York City for four years. Now he was in São Paolo, Brazil, teaching at the American School. It was after midnight, and Lustick was watching President Bill Clinton's State of the Union speech on television. "To have the best schools, we must have the best teachers," the president said as he endorsed the National Board for Professional Teaching Standards (NBPTS).

Clinton noted that just 500 of the nation's three million teachers had been certified by NBPTS as accomplished veteran teachers since 1994, the first year of credentialing. He asked Congress to provide the resources to encourage 100,000 teachers to become National Board certified in the coming years. "We should reward and recognize our best teachers. And as we reward them, we should quickly and fairly remove those few who don't measure up, and we should challenge more of our finest young people to consider teaching as a career."

That was the first time David Lustick heard of National Board certification. The idea grabbed him: "I felt that my practice was unrecognized. This was a way to distinguish myself and improve my marketability for future positions." Later that year, Lustick paid the $2,000-plus fee out of his own pocket and began the process of getting National Board certification to teach high school science.

During the next seven months he prepared a 140-page portfolio of essays, sample lessons, and student work aimed at demonstrating his ability to plan lessons, teach strategies of scientific inquiry, and lead productive classroom discussions. Added to the portfolio were two 20-minute videos of Lustick at work in the classroom. Finally, he flew to Miami for an all-day test of his science knowledge through six written exercises.

Fewer than half of that year's applicants succeeded; Lustick was among them. It turned out to be a highlight of his young career—a rich professional development experience that increased his understanding of his own strengths and weaknesses as well as his confidence. "I felt much more empowered both as a teacher and as an individual. The process really forced me to stop and look at my work, to think about my performance in the classroom, to consider how students might experience my lessons—something I took for granted—and to ask, 'Is this really the best I can do?'" he says.

Since 1987, 44 states and 280 school districts have invested tens of millions of dollars to encourage teachers to try for Board certification. By the end of 2001, 16,037 teachers were National Board certified in 19 areas ranging from Early Childhood/Generalist to Adolescence and Young Adult/Mathematics. In 2002, 20,202 teachers applied for certification. Based on 2001 results, more than half were expected to succeed at the end of the 10-month process, for a total of more than 26,000 teachers—a long stride toward the Board's mark of certifying 100,000 teachers by 2006.

Why the increasing interest? Some teachers, like Lustick, do it for the challenge and enhanced prestige. Others respond to financial incentives such as bonuses and better pay. Still others expect to use the credential as a springboard to leadership positions within the teacher ranks. For most candidates, the draw is probably a combination of all three incentives.

Although just one-half of one percent of the nation's teachers are certified, their influence is greater than the numbers suggest. For one thing, they are helping to shape an emerging consensus among education professionals about what defines teacher quality. For another, they comprise a powerful constituency of professionals who demonstrate an ability and willingness to articulate those standards to their colleagues. Ninety-three percent of candidates—both successful and unsuccessful—say they believe the Board certification process has made them better teachers. Almost as many say the process taught them to create stronger curricula (89%) and improved their ability to evaluate student learning (89%).

Like most school reform efforts of the past two decades, the program began in the wake of *A Nation at Risk*, the 1983 federal report that decried the state of U.S. schools. As a result, the Carnegie Forum on Education and the Economy put together its Task Force on Teaching as a Profession. Its 1987 report, *A Nation Prepared: Teachers for the 21st Century*, suggested creating a voluntary system of national certification comparable to the medical profession's licensing procedures.

With the financial backing of Carnegie and other foundations, the major teachers unions, and the U.S. Department of Education, the NBPTS was launched as a private, nonprofit organization led by an all-star roster of advisors from the fields of policy, research, and practice. Drafting comprehensive, research-based standards and assessments took almost five years. The result was a widely praised credentialing system with broad support in the ranks of education professionals. Indeed, two major licensing bodies for graduates of teacher-education programs—the National Council for Accreditation of Teacher Education (NCATE) and the Interstate New Teacher Assessment and Support Consortium (INTASC)—have aligned their standards with the National Board's.

The Board has helped spark a national conversation among teachers about what constitutes good practice, an effort that aims to let teachers take control and "own" the discussion about teaching standards. To get certified, teachers must be able to explain and demonstrate their classroom practices—via ten written entries and two classroom videos—in a way that satisfies the expectations of scorers in the national office.

"This [process] has given teachers a structured environment in which to develop and use a vocabulary of good practice," says Jill Harrison Berg, a Board-certified humanities teacher in the Cambridge (Mass.) public schools. "The process is really an intensive professional development exercise. It requires teachers to explain the choices they make in their practice—and that means they have to learn to be articulate about teaching."

TOUGH QUESTIONS

Yet for all its positive reviews, both supporters and skeptics of Board certification are pressing for answers to tough questions. Do students learn more in classes taught by Board-certified teachers? Do low-performing schools benefit in any measurable way? Why do the passing rates of minority NBPTS candidates trail those of whites by wide margins? Is the assessment biased against teachers who employ more traditional, teacher-centered instructional methods? In other words, has the $200 million investment of charitable and taxpayer funds in this credentialing system been worthwhile?

The Board isn't shying away from these and other issues. In fact, it recently brought more than 200 scholars to Chicago to discuss what research would not only address the concerns of critics but improve the process. At the conference, NBPTS officials invited proposals from all quarters of the education research community and pledged to raise millions of dollars to fund new studies.

One study already completed supports the contention that Board-certified teachers are more capable, on average, than those who aren't—at least as measured by NBPTS criteria. Researchers, led by Lloyd Bond of the University of North Carolina–Greensboro, compared the practice of 31 teachers who won certification with that of 34 teachers who failed the process. They observed each teacher in class for about 75 hours, interviewed both teachers and students, and examined lesson plans. In addition, four students from each class were randomly asked to submit samples of their work for evaluation. All 65 teachers—drawn from North Carolina, Ohio, and Washington, D.C.—had similar education and experience.

"The differences we observed were pervasive, compelling, and consistent," the researchers wrote. National Board–certified teachers did a better job in 11 of 13 categories, including improvising and adapting lessons as situations dictate, critiquing their own performance, articulating high standards, designing lessons aligned to those standards, and showing a deep knowledge of their subject. They showed more enthusiasm for teaching, and in two categories—understanding verbal and nonverbal responses of children, and offering feedback to students—the Board-certified teachers also performed better, but not by statistically significant margins.

BETTER EDUCATIONS?

Critics noted, however, that the students' academic performance got little or no consideration in the Bond study. National Board officials hope a new study of North Carolina's Board-certified teachers can find a concrete link between Board certification and improved student learning. William P. Sanders, head of assessment services for SAS in School, a North Carolina–based research and development firm, will apply his "value-added" method in examining the work of Board-certified teachers in North Carolina.

The purpose of value-added assessment is to quantify in a concrete way the impact that teachers have on their individual students by examining the progress (or lack thereof) those students make over several years on standardized tests. The method enables researchers to identify the years in which student achievement grew, shrank, or stayed the same. Doing so gives a better picture of teacher effectiveness than simply averaging test scores, Sanders contends. If, say, a student in a sixth-grade class scores well above average while another scores at rock bottom—just as they did the previous year—combining their scores might suggest an acceptable, if not spectacular, performance by the teacher. A value-added analysis would reveal that neither student made progress in the teacher's class.

In Tennessee, Sanders concluded that the connection posited by many researchers between students' academic performance and such factors as socioeconomic status was not as important as teacher effectiveness. "I can adjust for race, socioeconomic status, school location, [and] class size, and come up with different results," he says. "The one thing that you can never hide is teacher quality. It is the single most important factor."

Critics of Sanders's work argue that even the best teachers may not be able to compensate for lack of family involvement, class size, students' prior knowledge, and other factors. And then there's the fact that Sanders's method relies on standardized tests, which some would say don't necessarily tell what students have learned in a particular class but what they have learned from all sources, including family, friends, and media.

Sanders has rich soil for his North Carolina project: the state has 3,660 Board-certified teachers, the most among the states and nearly a quarter of the national total. That is due in part to generous incentives. Board-certified teachers get 12 percent more than their noncertified peers from the state; in districts like Charlotte-Mecklenburg they get another 10 percent on top of that. In addition, North Carolina administers end-of-grade standardized tests for students in grades 3–8 and end-of-course tests for high schoolers, providing a significant body of data for Sanders to analyze.

ADVERSE IMPACT

Another top research priority for the National Board is to reduce the discrepancy in pass rates between white teachers and
teachers of color. While 53 percent of white candidates for certification passed in 2001, just 22 percent of African Americans and 38 percent of Hispanics did. Is there some bias hidden in the portfolio assignments? Or in the way portfolios are
scored? The Board asked UNC–Greensboro's Lloyd Bond, a
respected African American researcher, to look for answers.
He conducted a small study and found nothing in the process
itself to account for the discrepancy. "Rather, adverse impact
may well be traceable to more systemic factors in U.S. society
at large," he concluded, and suggested more research.

Gloria Ladson-Billings of the University of Wisconsin–Milwaukee and Linda Darling-Hammond of Stanford University
took up the issue, looking at how the work of urban teachers
of color gets evaluated by teacher assessment programs, including the National Board's. According to the researchers,
these teachers face significant obstacles to becoming NBPTS
certified. They don't get as much institutional support, incentives, and collegial encouragement to pursue certification as
their white counterparts typically do. Also, they tend to teach
a greater proportion of underachieving students, teach in isolation with fewer professional development opportunities,
and have less familiarity with the formats and requirements
of such assessments.

Furthermore, the researchers' review of educational literature on what constitutes "good teaching" revealed that such
definitions do not include some of the skills and strategies
employed by successful teachers of urban students of color.

Research shows that such teachers usually make special efforts to develop caring relationships with students—sometimes in a way that might appear too informal, too "parental" to outsiders. These teachers also improvise ways of delivering curricula that might otherwise be out of sync with the students' cultures, experiences, and communication patterns.

"But how is a sense of caring and cultural solidarity exhibited in an assessment? What words, gestures, pieces of evidence can be collected that demonstrate the connection between a teacher and her students?" asked Ladson-Billings and Darling-Hammond in a report written for the National Partnership for Excellence and Accountability in Teaching. Since the NBPTS assessment doesn't appear to take into account such relationships, some of the methods employed by urban teachers might not be measurable by scorers at the national office.

CONTENT VS. PEDAGOGY

Of course, disagreements about defining good teaching are not limited to questions of racial and cultural differences. For example, the Board has been especially criticized for overemphasizing teaching methods at the expense of content knowledge. Michael Poliakoff of the National Council on Teacher Quality (NCTQ) is one such critic. "[The National Board] doesn't encourage mastery of subjects as it should, nor does it ask teachers to show that their teaching translates into student achievement," he says. "A master teacher has to be a master at getting results. The process of teaching doesn't matter so much if you don't know what you're teaching and if students don't learn."

The NCTQ, which is based in Falls Church, Va., has partnered with the nine-state Education Leaders Council to develop its own advanced certification for veteran teachers and alternative certification for new teachers with $5 million in seed money from the U.S. Department of Education. The new American Board for Certification of Teacher Excellence will certify teachers based on how well they and their students perform on standardized tests.

A different but related concern is raised by Robert Burroughs, assistant professor in the College of Education at the University of Cincinnati, who notes that the process "may be as much an evaluation of a teacher's writing about his or her teaching practice as it is an evaluation of the teaching itself." Burroughs, who has coached more than 100 candidates for NBPTS certification at all grade levels, writes in the *Journal of Teacher Education* that "candidates must solve a number of rhetorical problems" in the course of preparing a portfolio. "Like a club, NBPTS has a particular way of talking (standards) and a particular way of doing (portfolio formats)," he writes. "Because these particular ways are often unfamiliar, candidates can often feel like outsiders, vulnerable to worries about adequacy and susceptible to bouts of defensiveness."

Burroughs points out that some candidates have trouble imagining their audience. Who are the unseen, unknown judges that will read this stuff? Some teachers also question whether they can adequately capture the complexity and dynamics of their practice in writing, such as the "tacit knowledge" earned through years in the classroom. Are all excellent teachers articulate about their practice? Are all those who are articulate about their practice excellent teachers?

BOARD GAMES?

Questions about performance also raise concerns about cutting corners in the application process. Michael Podgursky, an economist at the University of Missouri–Columbia, has argued that long-distance judging of applications makes cheating more likely. He points out that no input is requested from local school administrators who know the applicants and their work—a significant departure from the medical model in which supervising physicians weigh in on a young doctor's competence.

Staging video performances is another concern, says Brent Stephens, a Boston elementary school teacher who was certified in 2001. Stephens says that, in his experience, teachers and their coaches discussed removing all but the best-behaved kids from a class before shooting video. "It ought to be appalling to anybody," he says, "but a lot of teachers did it. So you see these videos of eight quiet kids in a conspicuously empty classroom. That sort of thing wasn't discouraged. And as more people get certified and help each other, the opportunities for gaming the system will grow."

Ann Harman, director of research and information at NBPTS, says that cheating is no surprise but also not a great concern. "Any testing program has its cheaters, and we deal with them harshly. Anyone caught cheating is disqualified for life." She also questions whether removing certain kids would be effective: "It's not a strategy I would recommend because it doesn't give you the best opportunity to show what you can do. In fact, highlighting classes where students may present a difficult challenge is a better strategy to demonstrate competence."

POLICY ISSUES

While the NBPTS tries to work out its research and logistical questions, a number of practical issues challenge policymakers. Since its inception, the Board has focused on identifying what it considers master teachers, leaving questions about how that designation is used to state and local school boards, says Susan Moore Johnson, Pforzheimer Professor of Teaching and Learning at the Harvard Graduate School of Education. In the highly localized landscape of U.S. education, a national credential takes on very different meaning from district to district, especially in terms of teacher pay, recruitment, retention, and promotion (see sidebar).

As the number of National Board–certified teachers grows, national and local policymakers, union leaders, and K–12 administrators will have to decide what practical meaning such a certification should have:

- Will it become a nationally portable credential, so that teachers can pursue opportunities in new districts rather than going to the back of the line with each new job they take? Johnson points out that although most U.S. professions reward mobility, teaching stymies it because of localized contracts.
- Will the present level of financial support and big bonuses from states and districts continue? In 2001, Virginia cut back its bonus to newly certified teachers from $5,000 to about $1,632 and its annual salary bonus from $2,500 to $816, disappointing many who had been drawn by the pay increase.
- Will affluent districts poach teachers with bonuses that poorer districts can't match? In Virginia, Board-certified

RULES OF ATTRACTION

The incentives and rewards for pursuing National Board certification vary from state to state, district to district. For example, the San Francisco Unified School District offers a candidate support program and a $5,000 annual bonus for the 10-year life of the certificate. Neighboring Oakland pays $500 toward the NBPTS fee and provides assistance for the videotaping; those who teach at low-performing schools can earn a $5,000 annual bonus from the state for four years. Other examples:

- Austin, Tex.: National Board–certified teachers (NBCTs) receive an annual $2,000 pay raise and can earn another $1,000 a year for extra work, such as mentoring. They keep the raise even if promoted out of teaching into professional or administrative positions within the district.
- Cherokee County, N.C.: Lends candidates laptop computers. Those who achieve certification keep the computers as long as they remain an employee of the Cherokee County schools. In addition, all NBCTs get a 12 percent pay raise from the state. In July 2004, the state agreed to pay the certification fee up front and provide three days of leave time for candidate preparations.
- Colonial, Del.: Gives each NBCT a $500 voucher for classroom materials. (State pays most of the application fee.) An interest-free loan program is also available for NBCT candidates.
- Coventry, R.I.: Successful candidates get a $6,500 annual stipend, which increases to $7,000 in the 2003–04 school year. The district also provides use of video, editing, and computer equipment. (State pays most of the application fee.)

- Denali Borough, Alaska: Provides leave time and substitute teachers for candidates. (State may pay part of application fee.)
- Washoe County, Nev.: Candidates get three days' paid leave for portfolio preparation. Successful ones get an 8 percent raise for the life of the certificate. (State pays most of the application fee.)

Source: NBPTS

teachers who may lose their state bonus money might be tempted to move to higher-paying districts like Fairfax County. On the other hand, some districts are using bonuses to attract teachers to schools that need the most help: in San Francisco, teachers can earn $80,000 in bonus money over the course of 10 years for working in low-performing schools.

Think of all the measures taken in the past two decades to improve U.S. schools: changes in administrative structures, in testing and assessment, in curricula and standards, in school schedules, in graduation requirements and promotion policies. The effort to ensure that teachers—those who actually spend their days with students—are highly skilled and motivated to improve their practice is arguably the most important measure communities can support.

Early research suggests that National Board certification may be a way to do so. Its requirements are certainly more rigorous than those of standard certification programs. At the same time, it can give teachers, who so often practice in isolation, the opportunity to join a larger community of practitioners and have a say in the national dialogue on what constitutes good teaching. But like all reform measures, the success or failure of Board certification will depend on how one question gets answered: What's in it for students—and not just in well-off communities but in poor ones, too?

This chapter originally appeared in the March/April 2002 issue of the Harvard Education Letter.

Note: Since this article was originally published, two studies have confirmed that National Board certification is an effective indicator of teacher quality. A study by Arizona State University researchers, released in September 2004, compared the academic performance of students taught by Board-certified and non-Board-certified teachers in 35 elementary classrooms across 14 school districts between 1999–2003. They found that students taught by Board-certified teachers made greater gains than students taught by non-Board-certified teachers in almost 75 percent of the comparisons (Vandevoort, Amrein-Beardsley, & Berliner, 2004). Similarly, a study by the CNA Corporation for the National Science Foundation and National Board for Professional Teaching Standards, released in November 2004, examined 108,000 student records from the Miami-Dade County Public Schools to assess the impact of Board certification on student gains in mathematics in the ninth and tenth grades. It found that students with otherwise similar teachers made larger gains if their teachers were Board certified (Cavalluzzo, 2004).

REFERENCES

Cavalluzzo, L. C. (2004, November). *Is National Board certification an effective signal of teacher quality?* Alexandria, VA: CNA Corporation. Available online at www.cna.org/expertise/education.

Vandevoort, L. G., Amrein-Beardsley, A. & Berliner, D. C. (2004, September 8). National Board certified teachers and their students' achievement. *Education Policy Analysis Archives, 12*(46). Available online at http://epaa.asu.edu/epaa/v12n46/.

FOR FURTHER INFORMATION

L. Bond. "Culturally Responsive Pedagogy and the Assessment of Accomplished Teaching." *Journal of Negro Education* 67, no. 3 (1998): 242–254.

R. Burroughs. "Composing Standards and Composing Teachers." *Journal of Teacher Education* 52, no. 3 (May/June 2001): 222–223.

R. Burroughs, T.A. Schwartz, and M. Hendricks-Lee. "Communities of Practice and Discourse Communities: Negotiating Boundaries in NBPTS Certification." *Teachers College Record* 102, no. 2 (April 2000): 346–376.

Carnegie Task Force on Teaching as a Profession. "A Nation Prepared: Teachers for the 21st Century." New York: Carnegie Forum on Education and the Economy, 1986.

S.M. Johnson. "Can Professional Certification for Teachers Reshape Teaching as a Career?" *Phi Delta Kappan* 82, no. 5 (January 2001): 393–399.

G. Ladson-Billings. *The Dreamkeepers: Successful Teachers of African American Children*. San Francisco: Jossey-Bass, 1994.

G. Ladson-Billings and L. Darling-Hammond. "The Validity of National Board for Professional Teaching Standards (NBPTS)/ Interstate New Teacher Assessment and Support Consortium (INTASC) Assessments for Effective Urban Teachers: Findings and Implications for Assessments." Paper prepared for the National Partnership for Excellence and Accountability in Teaching, May 2000.

National Board for Professional Teaching Standards. 1525 Wilson Blvd., Suite 500, Arlington, VA 22209; tel: 703-465-2700; fax: 703-465-2715. www.nbpts.org

National Board for Professional Teaching Standards. *What Teachers Should Know and Be Able to Do*. Arlington, VA: NBPTS, 1999.

M. Podgursky. "Should States Subsidize National Certification?" *Education Week*, April 11, 2001, pp. 38, 40–41.

CHAPTER 10

School-Based Coaching

A revolution in professional development— or just the latest fad?

By Alexander Russo

> "They call it coaching, but it is teaching. You do not just tell them it is so. You show them the reasons why it is so."
> —*Vince Lombardi*

After years of disappointing results from conventional professional development efforts and under ever-increasing accountability pressures, many districts are now hiring coaches to improve their schools. These coaches don't use locker-room pep talks to motivate their teams, but they do strive to improve morale and achievement—and raise scores—by showing teachers how and why certain strategies will make a difference for their students.

The professional development strategy known as school-based coaching generally involves experts in a particular subject area or set of teaching strategies working closely with small groups of teachers to improve classroom practice and, ultimately, student achievement. In some cases coaches work full-time at an individual school or district; in others they work with a variety of schools throughout the year. Most are former classroom teachers, and some keep part-time classroom duties while they coach.

In the United States, school-based coaching was pioneered primarily in large districts like Boston and New York City's Community School District #2, and it has been spreading quickly around the nation, particularly in urban schools. Examples of these efforts include:

- New York City's public schools recently embarked on a large-scale staff development effort to support reading, writing, and math programs, assigning experienced coaches to schools throughout the city. The coaches will not only work with small groups of teachers during planning time but also set up demonstration classrooms where teachers can watch sample lessons that they can later replicate with their own students.

- In Philadelphia, a group of schools was chosen to pilot a coaching program during the 2002–03 school year as part of a school restructuring effort. Each coach worked part-time at several schools, and first-year results were strong enough that, in August 2003, Philadelphia contracted with the *Princeton Review* to create and implement a professional development program for approximately 500 school-based instructional leaders and 130 coaching staff. The goal is to provide district educators with the skills and tools necessary to monitor student performance more closely and to help shape classroom instruction based on individual student performance data.

- In Dallas, former associate superintendent and "reading czar" Robert B. Cooter Jr. emphasized the need for literacy coaches as part of his districtwide Dallas Reading Plan to improve student performance. To attract the best staff developers to Dallas schools, Cooter persuaded a local foundation to provide a $10,000 per year stipend to supplement each literacy coach's district salary. By 2001, five years after the program began, all of the schools involved had been removed from the state's low-performing list and student reading performance had improved dramatically. "We got the best of the best," Cooter told the *St. Louis Post-Dispatch* in 2003.

- America's Choice, a school reform model used in roughly 600 schools in 15 states, includes a strong school-based coaching component. Teachers work with math and literacy coaches one-on-one and in small groups to develop instructional strategies and to build model classrooms for innovative language arts and mathematics programs.

A PROFESSIONAL DEVELOPMENT ALTERNATIVE

One of the most compelling rationales for school-based coaching is that many of the more conventional forms of professional development—such as conferences, lectures, and mass teacher-institute days—are unpopular with educators because they are often led by outside experts who tell teachers what to do, then are never heard from again. To be effective, scores of researchers say, professional development must be ongoing, deeply embedded in teachers' classroom work with children, specific to grade levels or academic content, and focused on research-based approaches. It also must help to open

COACHING MEETS STANDARDS
FOR EFFECTIVE STAFF DEVELOPMENT

School-based coaching meets many of the standards set forth by the National Staff Development Council (NSDC), the nation's largest professional association dedicated to improving teacher professional development. Recommendations in the latest NSDC standards, adopted in 2001 (and summarized here), include:

- the organization of educators into "learning communities" that have clear goals consistent with school and district goals
- effective leadership to support "continuous instructional improvement"
- the application of research to school and classroom strategies and decisionmaking
- support for teacher collaboration
- the development of educators' skills at increasing parent involvement

To view the NSDC standards online, see www.nsdc.org/standards/index.cfm

classroom doors and create more collaboration and sense of community among teachers in a school.

When compared with many other approaches, school-based coaching seems to meet many of these criteria remarkably well. It also seems to meet many of the standards set forth by the National Staff Development Council, the country's largest professional association dedicated to improving teacher professional development (see sidebar). Coaching at its best is focused on authentic student work, is closely tied to a specific school or district's curriculum and to teachers' practice, takes place on a continuous basis, and relies heavily on research.

"Instead of everyone going out and hearing an expert speak who is not familiar with Boston, coaches are now becoming the experts," says Gemina Gianino, a former classroom teacher who is now lead literacy coach at two elementary schools in the Boston Public Schools system. Gianino, who "coaches the coaches" at the city's Mary Lyon and Harvard-Kent schools, has attended her share of single-day professional development presentations and workshops and believes coaching is superior to these one-shot approaches because it helps provide something that's on every educator's mind these days: accountability.

"When you go to a workshop for a day, you come back and no one's holding you accountable. You might get credit for going out to that workshop, but no one was there with you to say, 'Now how do we make what you learned work in here?'" Gianino notes. "And so here we're saying, 'We're with you through this. We're not only helping you figure out what it is, but we're going to stay with you while you figure it out. We're not just going to give you advice and then leave.'" As Gianino points out, one of a coach's main goals is to make certain that the ideas a teacher gains in the professional development setting are translated into actions that have a chance to improve student learning.

COACHING CAVEATS

Despite the apparent promise and newfound popularity of school-based coaching, experts say school leaders should think carefully before hopping on the coaching bandwagon. First, there are tremendous variations in what people call "coaching"—educators should be clear about their goals and expectations before making an investment in any type of coaching initiative.

Alan Richard, a state policy writer for *Education Week*, authored a May 2003 report on school-based staff development for the Edna McConnell Clark Foundation. After conducting interviews and observations at local schools and reviewing coaching literature, Richard describes the practice of coaching as a "promising but often poorly focused school improvement tactic." He also notes that school leaders who expect coaching alone to solve a host of problems, from low test scores to poor student-teacher relationships, are setting themselves up for disappointment.

"I saw too many examples where the coaching wasn't enough," Richard says. "Most of what I saw showed that coaches could help a school improve, but not alone, and not without attention to other pressing issues, such as broader efforts in professional development, learning environment, leadership, resources, use of technologies, community involvement in the school, well-developed and thoughtful curricula, etc."

Another report by the Consortium for Policy Research in Education (CPRE) says school-based coaching fills "a particular and promising niche" in the larger scope of school districts' improvement efforts. "Coaching is increasingly relied upon by schools and districts across the nation to train teachers on a particular set of instructional techniques and practices," the CPRE authors write. They also concede, however, that the evidence of coaching's success is largely anecdotal and that the research base in support of coaching is woefully small: "Few, if any, studies provide evidence that coaching strategies, in whatever form, lead to greater student learning."

There are also numerous logistical challenges associated with implementing school-based coaching on a large scale, these experts say. These challenges include finding enough good coaches without draining schools of their most successful teachers, training and supporting coaches so that they have a clear notion of what they are supposed to be doing, and dedicating enough time in the school day so that coaching can be effective.

The first challenge—finding enough coaches—can be a major obstacle in some districts. Barbara Neufeld, former lecturer at the Harvard Graduate School of Education and president of the education research agency Education Matters, points out that in Boston and San Diego "neither district can find as many coaches as they need, and [the task is] much more difficult in math than in literacy."

Training and support for coaches is yet another challenge, since site-based professional developers need their own professional development. In Boston, for example, lead literacy coaches like Gianino work in a small number of schools to train the coaches within those buildings.

Securing teacher release time and buy-in to participate in the coaching enterprise—whether coaching or being coached—is another issue. In at least some cases, officials are "underestimating what it takes to do the work, the implications of removing these people from schools, and what it would take to train them," says Neufeld, who has studied coaching efforts in Boston, San Diego, and Louisville.

There is also the issue of cost. Boston had spent almost $6 million on its coaching program, which included 75 coaches in 97 schools, as of Neufeld's 2003 report. So far, in nearly all cases, outside funds have been critical to getting coaching programs up and running. Places like Chicago and Boston have conducted "audits" of their professional development spending to figure out how best to monitor and coordinate their efforts.

Finally, there are a number of cultural challenges created by coaching. In many situations, the coach's role in a school is almost entirely new and different—he or she is neither administrator nor district overseer nor classroom peer. Schools and school systems are simply not used to these positions. Perhaps more important, teachers are not usually accustomed to talking about their work in the way one does when working with a coach.

For these reasons and others, schools and districts need to make an institutional commitment to coaching in order for it to have any hope of succeeding, says Ellen Guiney, director of the Boston Plan for Excellence, a local education fund that partnered with the Boston Public Schools to develop the city's Collaborative Coaching and Learning (CCL) model. Guiney says the program has evolved since its 1996 inception, as coaches and district leaders have learned the drawbacks of not having a coherent and systematic plan. "We initially started out [only] having coaches work with teacher volunteers, and we wasted a lot of time. If the school's leadership doesn't support [coaches] and the staff doesn't see them being supported, then the coaches are wasted," Guiney says. "Teachers have a lot to do. Time has to be set aside, they need support, and they need to see the work as worthwhile."

In response to these kinds of concerns, Boston's initial one-day-a-week, one-teacher-at-a-time coaching model has now been replaced by revolving six- to eight-week "cycles" that school leaders and teachers both have a say in scheduling. During a cycle, a coach visits a group of between four and ten teachers at a school twice a week, working alongside them in their own classrooms as the teams demonstrate, observe, and reflect upon effective instructional practices.

WHAT NEXT?

Most immediately, better school-based coaching research is needed. Teacher surveys and evaluation studies have thus far lagged well behind the interest in and implementation of coaching programs. Without adequate research, says Neufeld, "there isn't any way of knowing in fact whether [coaching] is worth the money."

At the same time, districts need to be sure that they are implementing quality programs that they can support. In some cases, says Richard, "leaders have not invested the time, thought, and resources necessary to launch and sustain a coherent program and to address other serious problems within schools or districts that create barriers for in-school staff developers."

Still, both the spotty track record of traditional professional development and the success stories that have emerged from coaching so far suggest that this new strategy may have a great deal of untapped potential. At least in theory, school-based coaching helps educators envision a world where professional development means showing and not telling; where teachers can learn and improve their practice in a reflective, supportive setting; and where coaches serve as liaisons between research and practice, bringing the latest findings to where they are most needed—the classroom.

"[Coaching] offers long-term follow-up, long-term consistency, and a sense of trust so that you can go in and be a supportive agent for the classroom teacher," says Pat Butler, lead coach at Boston's Perry and Marshall elementary schools. "If [teachers'] skills are sharpened, then they are going to transfer this information into their classroom, and both their practice and their students will benefit."

This chapter originally appeared in the July/August 2004 issue of the Harvard Education Letter.

FOR FURTHER INFORMATION

Boston Plan for Excellence in the Public Schools, 6 Beacon St., Suite 615, Boston, MA 02108; tel: 617-227-8055. www.bpe.org

D. Burney, T.B. Corcoran, and J. Lesnick. "A Review of Research on Instructional Coaching" (working title). Philadelphia: Consortium for Policy Research in Education, University of Pennsylvania (forthcoming).

B. Neufeld and D. Roper. "Coaching: A Strategy for Developing Instructional Capacity: Promises and Practicalities." Washington, DC: Aspen Institute Program on Education and Annenberg Institute for School Reform, 2003. Available online at www.edmatters.org/webreports/CoachingPaperfinal.pdf

S.M. Poglinco, A.J. Bach, K. Hovde, S. Rosenblum, M. Saunders, and J.A. Supovitz. "The Heart of the Matter: The Coaching Model in America's Choice Schools." Philadelphia: Consortium for Policy Research in Education, University of Pennsylvania, 2003. Available online at www.cpre.org/Publications/Publications_Research.htm

A. Richard. "Making Our Own Road: The Emergence of School-Based Staff Developers in America's Public Schools." New York: Edna McConnell Clark Foundation, 2003. Available online at www.emcf.org/programs/student/student_pub.htm

CHAPTER 11

Collaborative Teacher Evaluation

Putting the focus where it should be—
on student improvement

By Louise Kennedy

amen Lopez, principal of Los Penasquitos Elementary School in San Diego, Calif., met recently with a teacher for an annual evaluation. The meeting followed his usual pattern. Before the meeting, Lopez gave the teacher a packet of student performance data from the previous year. The data showed how the students performed on recent tests and how these results compared with those of last year's students, the grade-level goals, and the school as a whole, as well as how much each student had improved.

During these meetings, Lopez always asks teachers what patterns the data show, what strengths students exhibited, what challenges might lie ahead for their students, and how this information may influence their teaching.

"I'll give the data to them, and basically they drive the conversation," Lopez says.

In this case, the teacher noticed that the whole class was struggling with fractions. Lopez suggested she consult with another teacher who had a strong reputation for effective teaching. Within a half-hour, the two teachers had set up a time to talk. "I was really pleased," Lopez says.

Principals like Lopez are convinced that it is this process of reviewing concrete results together that helps teachers improve—and transforms the principal's role. "It's very powerful when they can see [the results] themselves, and I can serve as a facilitator," Lopez says. "We need that discovery to come from them as individuals, because that's what's going to drive the most meaningful change."

This is what effective teacher supervision and evaluation looks like today—a collaborative process that places teacher and principal side by side, looking at results and finding practical ways to improve, says Jo Blase, coauthor of *Handbook of Instructional Leadership: How Successful Principals Promote Teaching and Learning*. Blase and her research partner, fellow University of Georgia professor of educational leadership Joseph Blase, stress that principals need to find ways to put learning at the center of what they do every day. As research increasingly supports the idea that the most effective principals are "instructional leaders," rather than bureaucratic managers, principals are finding new ways to put that idea into practice.

FROM ADMINISTRATORS TO FACILITATORS

In recent years, there has been a fundamental shift in how principals see their relationships with teachers, says Richard Elmore, Gregory R. Anrig Professor of Educational Leadership at the Harvard Graduate School of Education. Since the turn of the 19th century, Elmore says, principals in the United

States have largely seen themselves as bureaucratic administrators—in contrast to the British model of a "principal teacher," a first among equals who works with teachers as an expert colleague. Even though our own principals take their name from this model, Elmore argues, the content of their jobs has done little to reflect it.

Until now. With the accountability movement putting intense pressure on school leaders to improve academic performance, American principals are once again defining themselves increasingly as teachers who manage other teachers, rather than managers removed from the business of teaching. And as they do so, they are focusing not so much on how well teachers teach as on how well students learn.

Daniel Gutekanst's philosophy on supervision reflects this trend. Before coming to Shrewsbury, Mass., where he has been principal of Shrewsbury High School for 10 years, Gutekanst worked on a Connecticut team that evaluated new teachers. That program followed a traditional approach of relying on formulaic checklists of teacher practices (for example, writing assignments on the board), the results of which were then tabulated by a supervisor. In his own school, Gutekanst prefers a more collaborative approach that emphasizes collegial discussions among peers.

"We've turned our lens a little differently, to look at what the kids are doing," Gutekanst says. Instead of worrying about whether a teacher is writing on the blackboard or asking enough open-ended questions, Gutekanst focuses on evidence that the students are learning. When he observes classrooms, for instance, he watches the students more than the teacher. "I want to know that the students are engaged, that they're paying attention, that they're doing work, and what the work is," Gutekanst says. "To me the most important thing in the end is what the students are doing in the classroom, not what the teachers are doing."

PARTNERSHIPS AND TEAMS

"The interest has shifted from evidence of input and toward evidence of learning," agrees Richard DuFour, author of *Whatever It Takes: How Professional Learning Communities Respond When Kids Don't Learn* and former superintendent of Adlai E. Stevenson High School District 125 in Lincolnshire, Ill. Forming collaborative teams is critical for gathering such evidence and redesigning classroom practice in response to it, says DuFour. "The best way to help teachers enhance their instructional strategies isn't necessarily to have a principal drop in a few times a year, but to sit down with their colleagues, look at data, and figure out who's really learned how to teach a subject well," he says. In this kind of arrangement, instead of having a principal rate their performance, teachers are working with one another to improve their practice.

Working with collaborative teams of teachers also gives principals an opportunity to improve their evaluation methods. According to DuFour, "Principals are knocking themselves out trying to get in and evaluate teachers and spending hours and hours doing it." He argues that instead of spending 10 hours with one teacher, it makes more sense for a principal to spend 10 hours with a team of teachers. But, he notes, these kinds of partnerships "don't happen unless the principal creates all the systems and structures to make it happen."

At Shrewsbury High, Gutekanst has instituted a "collegial partners" program in which every teacher has a partner in another part of the school. The pairs make time at least twice a month to talk about teaching and learning, to visit each other's classrooms, and perhaps to design a lesson together. Partners talk about what is going on in their classrooms and look at student work together to figure out how both students' performance and the assessments themselves could be improved.

The faculty members, says Gutekanst, calls the collaborative pairs "Gute's buddies" or "forced friends." But as much as they tease Gutekanst about it, he is confident that teachers benefit from and enjoy these relationships. "It gets them out of their classroom and gets them talking about teaching. I know that if I just told them to do it, a few would, but most wouldn't. But when you actually expect it, people focus on it a little differently."

That kind of collaboration goes to the heart of what recent research defines as a principal's most important responsibilities: creating a shared culture of learning within a school, working collegially with teachers, and developing the structures and practices that encourage professional growth (see sidebar, p. 120). A recent analysis by Mid-Continent Research for Education and Learning, which looked at 70 studies of school leadership, identified these tasks as critical for principals. Also important, the study found, was that principals involve teachers in developing and implementing policy, rather than just imposing it from above.

Claire Crane, principal of Robert L. Ford Elementary School in Lynn, Mass., was reminded of the importance of teambuilding when her school decided a few years ago to go from a K–6 to a K–8 program. "I had to build a seventh-grade team and an eighth-grade team," Crane says. "Teambuilding is very, very important. You can't leave teachers in isolation."

ASK THE TEACHERS TO TEACH YOU:
SIX TIPS FOR PRINCIPALS

What can principals do to help teachers become more effective in their work? Most important, scholars say, is to move away from the traditional forms of supervision—observing classrooms and making check marks on a standardized list—and toward a more collegial, collaborative relationship with teachers. "The instruments that are typically used are too generic to be used for any useful instructional purpose, and the stakes are too high for the teachers," says Harvard Graduate School of Education professor Richard Elmore. "So that process becomes totally artificial and totally useless for both sides."

Instead, Elmore and others say, principals need to develop more individualized, deeper, and more professional ways of talking about teaching with their faculty. "You need to break into that culture and, in effect, ask the teachers to teach you how to become a better supervisor," Elmore says.

Some specific ideas:

1. Organize working teams around a specific problem: a group of students that needs extra help, a particular challenge in math or reading instruction, an area of concern that shows up through looking at test results.

2. Ask teachers what they need in order to teach more effectively: Schedule changes? Better access to research materials? More support from administrators or fellow teachers?

3. Find ways to minimize distractions. Some schools are hiring building managers so that principals can concentrate on instruction; even if that's not possible, a principal can delegate some mundane management tasks in order to free up time for working with teachers.

4. Don't expect traditional evaluation processes to provide enough feedback and communication with teachers about how to improve their work; instead, build discussions about teaching and learning into the regular schedule of work. But don't hesitate to use the process as a way of pushing teachers to improve or move on.

5. Share leadership. Setting up teams of teachers to work together and share knowledge about teaching can deepen their expertise without taking a principal's time, and it's an important part of providing instructional leadership.

6. Most important, see both teaching and educational leadership as professional practices, learn as much as possible about the state of the art, and continue to develop a shared culture of knowledge about what works and why.

It's not just a social issue, she notes. As DuFour says, "The challenge is to make sure that the teams focus on student learning." For Crane, as for many other principals in this standards-focused era, the process of making productive use of test results and other data has proven useful in building productive teams. On a recent staff development day, Crane says, the Ford faculty broke up by grade levels, then took all the students' test results in different subjects and analyzed them. After evaluating the results together, the group began to identify problems. "And we saw a common strand," Crane says: "'Gee, we know we have to work more on open response in each grade.' It was so helpful." The fact that the group arrived at this conclusion together, she says, rather than receiving a directive from on high, made all the difference.

CREATING A POSITIVE SCHOOL CLIMATE

Crane's willingness to work collaboratively with teachers has built staff loyalty and reduced turnover. But because she values a positive and supportive school culture, she also doesn't hesitate to get tough with teachers who are not doing a good job.

Edward Knopping, who teaches first grade at Peirce Elementary School in Newton, Mass., says that good teachers appreciate it when principals address those who aren't pulling their weight. "Teachers don't like mediocrity within their own building," he says. "A teacher that continues to be employed when that teacher really shouldn't be there—when that person finally is let go, or dealt with to become a better teacher, people are really relieved. The principal really needs to take the bull by the horns and address that."

Knopping, who has worked with several principals, gives the example of a successful principal who was known for direct communication. If one teacher complained about another, Knopping recalls, the principal would say, "Well, let's get that person in right away." He'd then tell the identified teacher, "Now this is what so-and-so has reported to me."

"The first time this happens to you, you're panting and sweating. But it's done with no judgment. And he made everything very clear, very open," Knopping says.

With countless obligations and distractions, does a principal have the time needed to develop these kinds of relationships with and among teachers? "You can find more time," says the University of Georgia's Blase, "by reprioritizing, delegating, focusing on what matters, changing how you use time in faculty meetings. Through the actual use of data and analysis, you get teachers working together on learning. Empower teachers to make decisions. Give teachers time to talk about teaching." In this way, leadership will become "more shared, more professional, more respectful, more productive," Blase says.

Or, as Knopping puts it, "The principal makes or breaks the school. He [or she] sets the work environment, sets the culture of the school. There are two cultures—what's written down, and then the business of what's really going on on a daily basis. And that's the principal."

CHAPTER 12

Preparing the "Highly Qualified Principal"

Will new training and recruitment programs reshape the profession?

By Alexander Russo

With its goal of putting a "highly qualified teacher" in every classroom, the 2002 No Child Left Behind Act (NCLB) has raised many questions about the current state of K–12 teacher preparation, certification, and professional development. Largely absent from the federal law are requirements about the qualifications of other school personnel, most notably principals. What if NCLB had also required that there be a "highly qualified principal" in every school? What would such a designation mean, and how would we prepare someone to be this kind of school leader?

In recent years, a small but growing number of school districts, state agencies, universities, and philanthropies have been grappling with these kinds of questions—rethinking the skills, preservice training, and professional support that go into creating a school leader who can spearhead effective classroom instruction. This newfound interest in nurturing the qualities of effective principalship stems from the growing realization of the crucial role principals play in supporting—or limiting—efforts to improve schools and raise student achievement. Most principals themselves would likely agree that plans to improve curriculum, integrate standards, implement schoolwide reform, or reduce the achievement gap often succeed or fail largely based on a school's leadership.

Yet the systems for preparing principals for U.S. schools have remained largely unchanged—and unquestioned—for many years. At the same time, high turnover rates in many regions have raised questions about whether there will even be *enough* candidates to lead schools effectively in the near future.

REVAMPING COURSEWORK

One aspect of principal preparation that is widely seen as "in need of improvement" is the academic coursework offered in certification programs. Many principals complain that their traditional university-based classroom training was too piecemeal, too generic, or too theoretical—not focused enough on real-world challenges such as turning schools around or leading teams of teachers. As Jill Budd, a sixth-year middle school principal in Duval County, Fla., recalls, "The majority of the coursework that I had was so theoretical that it never got around to the things you really need to know to run a school effectively."

The need for more practical principal training is one of the main findings of a 2003 report by the Center on Reinventing Public Education (CRPE) at the University of Washington. Based on interviews with more than 150 principals, the report found that universities generally provided them with a uniform set of courses that was often inappropriate for many of the schools they actually ended up leading. The report also found that principals do not necessarily have to be experts in every aspect of school life, but they must be skilled in diagnosing specific school needs and developing appropriate responses to those needs based on available resources—skills for which many of the principals interviewed believed their preservice training was inadequate.

In response to such concerns, some districts and universities have banded together to rethink traditional principal candidate coursework and replace it with programs that place greater emphasis on curriculum and instruction, the supervision of teachers, and professional development. In some places, the changes have been dramatic. At Oklahoma State University, for example, principal candidates must now take one-third of their courses in the area of curriculum and instruction. Previously, only one out of 12 courses was required in this area.

Some district leaders have even gone so far as to hire a liaison to help facilitate coordination between higher education institutions and their district, so that what is taught in university courses is related to what is needed most in a particular school or set of schools. Such training programs tailored to specific districts have tremendous benefits, according to some participants.

"The big difference is that you're really focusing on the culture of the district, using the language of the district," says Eric Markinson, an assistant principal at Churchill High School in Eugene, Ore., who participated in a district-specific principal-training program three years ago. "The homework projects were all situated in our schools and were specific to our school district, as opposed to having people from 30 different districts," he explains. The program, which also included a "critical friends" coaching element, was taught by local practitioners from Eugene schools, as well as university professors.

Other initiatives have gone even further in this direction. In the Principal Residency Network (PRN), a regional program that currently operates in New Hampshire, Vermont, Boston, and Providence, R.I., roughly 90 new principals have been trained to lead schools with virtually no traditional coursework, says codirector Dennis Littky. Using a modified "independent study" approach, the network relies on projects and assignments that are tailored to whatever areas candidates need to focus on most at their respective school sites. Each working with a director who is linked to a university-based certification program, candidates have to show that they have mastered a range of essential information and skills. If a candidate comes in with ten years' experience working extensively with parents, for example, then that person would work on areas such as budgeting and curriculum development.

Larry Myatt, a former mentor principal who now coordinates the program's Boston location, says the goal of the PRN is to give candidates "a pretty good dose of what it's like to be a principal." This real-world focus weeds out some who decide they aren't up for the challenge, he notes. "We get them as close as we can to the high wire," Myatt says. "We like the fact that we have a little bit of attrition in the program." The network's roughly 30 graduates, who receive state certification, advance based on the evaluation of the mentor principal and the university liaison.

WHO BECOMES A PRINCIPAL?

Another major change that some districts and states are making is to develop more proactive, purposeful recruiting methods for prospective principals, instead of the current "passive" system whereby teachers and others who are interested in administration essentially select themselves for leadership. These districts' leaders are looking for specific attributes in new principals. They actively recruit from among their ranks, then require that individuals apply to enter a training program, where candidates work on a specific set of competencies. Some of these efforts include the following:

- The Dallas Independent School District recently selected 25 aspiring school principals for a new training program, working in cooperation with the University of North Texas and the Southern Regional Education Board (SREB), an organization closely involved in helping districts in 16 southern states revamp their principal training and recruitment approaches. Recruitment focused on successful teachers with at least some experience working closely with other teachers and a "passion for improving student achievement," according to SREB senior vice president Gene Bottoms.

- In Springfield, Mass., the superintendent and other school leaders have developed a tailored program for district principals, for which they actively recruit people they believe can be effective school leaders. The district initiative has even encouraged the local university to revamp its own pro-

ALTERNATIVE PRINCIPAL CERTIFICATION: STATE OF THE STATES

The National Center for Education Information (NCEI), a private research organization that studies educator certification and recruitment, released a report in 2003 on the status of principal and superintendent certification in the U.S. Based on a survey of state officials responsible for school administrator licensure, NCEI reported that "alternative routes" for principal certification existed in the following states:

California	Massachusetts	New York
Hawaii	Minnesota	Ohio
Idaho	Mississippi	Oregon
Kentucky	New Hampshire	Tennessee
Maryland	New Jersey	Texas

According to NCEI, some of these programs allow for bringing leaders from outside the field of education into the ranks of the principalship, a practice that many education experts say does not work.

Thomas Toch, director of the Policy Forums program at the National Center on Education and the Economy, stops short of dismissing the practice altogether. He says, however, that merely "parachuting in" outsiders to be principals without adequate preparation and mentoring is a formula for failure.

"There's certainly a lot of talent to tap outside of education," Toch says. "But it's hard to come in from outside if you're not used to the culture of schools, the challenges of schooling, and what goes on in classrooms."

For Further Information

National Center for Education Information. "School Administrator Certification in the United States, State-by-State 2003." Available online at www.ncei.com/2003_Principals_Superintendents/Cover.pdf

gram, according to Richard Laine of the Wallace Foundation, which funds the Springfield project along with a host of other principal-training reforms around the country.

- In New York City, Chicago, Washington, D.C., and the San Francisco Bay Area, a small but innovative principal-training program called New Leaders for New Schools puts applicants through a rigorous prescreening process, which includes extensive interviews and role-playing exercises. The program accepts only a fraction of those who apply. In 2002, New Leaders received about 600 applications for 50 principal internships, according to cofounder Jon Schnur. New Leaders also has taken the controversial step of recruiting candidates from outside education, as long as they have a minimal amount of classroom experience.

Intentional or not, one notable effect of these efforts is that they often generate a more diverse group of candidates than is typical in the principal pool, according to SREB's Bottoms and others. This includes more women, some younger candidates, and many experienced teachers who may have considered becoming principals in the past, but had been reluctant to get "stuck" in the traditional assistant principal role of disciplinarian. In New York City, officials say that the first cohort of principals in training under the new program was 36 percent minority. According to New Leaders for New Schools officials, roughly half of its participants are minority candidates.

OBSTACLES TO CHANGE

As promising as they may be, these innovations in training and recruitment face serious obstacles before they can be adopted more widely. The current system has been in place for many years and provides a steady stream of tuition income to universities, as well as an open door for teachers to become certified as principals at a time when principal turnover is high.

There is also some debate about whether the principal should necessarily even *be* a school's primary instructional leader. Some envision a more management-oriented approach, with a stronger role for lead teachers in guiding instruction, or a shared leadership role that mirrors the chief executive officer/chief academic officer pairing currently being used in some large urban districts like San Diego and Chicago.

Other challenges include:

State certification issues. Many of the changes in how principals are trained are being made within current certification requirements and regulations, or through waivers, but nearly all revolve in some way around university-based training programs. More widespread change might require further adjustments to state certification requirements, either through regulatory changes or by statute (see sidebar).

Roughly 15 states have loosened their principal certification requirements over the past several years, according to the Wallace Foundation's Laine, but much more needs to be done. In New York City, for example, the district's Leadership Academy may, pending discussions with state officials, eventually certify its own principals rather than rely on an association with a higher education institution. "Universities have a lock on [principal] certification right now," Laine observes.

Professional development. Ongoing support and leadership development for principals is another key issue that must be addressed along with the training of new principals. One such effort, the National Institute for School Leadership (NISL), run by the National Center on Education and the Economy (NCEE), has made professional development for in-service principals its main focus. "You can have perhaps the biggest immediate impact on the quality of school leadership by working with those who are already drawing paychecks," says Thomas Toch, director of the NCEE's Policy Forums program.

Using ideas from the corporate world and from the National War College, which trains U.S. military leaders in Washington, D.C., the main idea behind the NISL is to "reorient" principals who are already on the job toward fully taking on the role of instructional leaders who can use student data effectively, identify weaknesses in order to improve student achievement, and reallocate resources accordingly. The program combines intensive instruction and online learning and is currently being implemented in a handful of districts.

Anecdotal reports are positive so far. "I've gotten professional development in the past," says Jill Budd of Duval County who—along with every other middle and high school principal in the district—participated in the two-year NISL program beginning in 2003. "But here [in the NISL program] there is a lot more opportunity to discuss issues with your peers."

Changing the workplace. Even the best-trained principals need a supportive workplace with reasonable expectations, and at least some of the new school leadership efforts are trying to address these kinds of concerns. Principal attrition rates are high, the pressures are tremendous, the level of real autonomy can be low, and the job is notoriously exhausting.

The New York City Leadership Academy program, as well as the performance-based system set up in the District of Columbia, are trying to make substantive changes so that principals can actually succeed at the reforms they have developed the skills to implement.

Up-front costs. One obvious factor common to many of these alternative or innovative training programs is that they require significant additional investments or reallocations by districts and foundations. Under the traditional system, candidates generally pay their own way, usually while teaching and receiving salary increases for additional graduate credits. No research exists at this point to prove that the added cost is making a difference, much less paying off. But one thing seems certain: without investments in leadership, real school reform faces an uphill battle.

"Cost is the biggest problem," says Dennis Littky of the Principal Residency Network. "This is unfortunate, because everybody should put their money into leadership."

This chapter originally appeared in the March/April 2004 issue of the Harvard Education Letter.

FOR FURTHER INFORMATION

E-Lead, c/o Institute for Educational Leadership, 1001 Connecticut Ave., NW, Suite 310, Washington, DC 20036; tel: 202-822-8405. www.e-lead.org

E. Gootman. "Schools Get $4 Million to Recruit Principals." *New York Times,* September 23, 2003, p. B4.

C. Mazzeo. "Improving Teaching and Learning by Improving School Leadership." Washington, DC: National Governors Association and NGA Center for Best Practices, September 2003. Available online at www.nga.org/cda/files/091203LEADERSHIP.pdf

National Institute for School Leadership, located at the National Center on Education and the Economy (NCEE), 555 13th St., NW, Suite 500 West, Washington, DC 20004; tel: 202-783-3668. www.ncee.org

Principal Residency Network, part of The Big Picture Company, 275 Westminster St., Suite 500, Providence, RI 02903; tel: 401-456-0600. www.bigpicture.org/WebSite2002NEW/PrincipalResidencyNetwork.htm

Southern Regional Education Board, 592 10th St., NW, Atlanta, GA 30318; tel: 404-875-9211. www.sreb.org

M. Stricherz. "In San Diego, Principals' Focus Is Teaching and Learning." *Education Week*, November 28, 2001, pp. 6–7.

About the Contributors

Katherine C. Boles is cofounder of the Learning/Teaching Collaborative, one of the country's first professional development schools, and Trilemma Solutions, an education consultancy (www.trilemmasolutions.com). She is also a lecturer on education at the Harvard Graduate School of Education. Boles writes and teaches about school reform, teacher education, and new forms of teacher leadership, and is an advocate for public policy changes to restructure the field of teaching. She is coauthor (with V. Troen) of *Who's Teaching Your Children? Why the Teacher Crisis Is Worse Than You Think and What Can Be Done About It* (2003).

Morgaen L. Donaldson is an advanced doctoral student at the Harvard Graduate School of Education and a researcher at the Project on the Next Generation of Teachers. She is a coauthor of *Finders and Keepers: Helping New Teachers Survive and Thrive in Our Schools* (2004) and coeditor of *Reflections of First-Year Teachers on School Culture: Questions, Hopes, and Challenges* (with R. Van Der Borgert and B. Poon, 1999). A former high school teacher, Donaldson was a founding faculty member of the Boston Arts Academy, Boston's public high school for the arts. She studies teachers' career development, professional growth, and current changes in rural schools.

David T. Gordon is editor of the best-selling book *The Digital Classroom: How Technology Is Changing the Way We Teach and Learn* (2000), and of the follow-up book, *Better Teaching and Learning in the Digital Classroom* (2003). Gordon is also the former editor of the *Harvard Education Letter* and winner of the 2003 National Press Club Award for newsletter journalism. He is currently director of communications at CAST, a nonprofit education research and development organization.

Pam Grossman is a professor at the Stanford University School of Education. Her teaching and research interests focus on the education of teachers, the relationship between teacher education, knowledge, and policy, and pragmatic issues related to teacher education. Grossman is coauthor of the forthcoming publication *Interdisciplinary Encounters: A Second Look*.

Susan M. Kardos is a senior research affiliate at the Project on the Next Generation of Teachers at the Harvard Graduate School of Education (HGSE) and a postdoctoral research fellow in education at the Mandel Center at Brandeis University. She received her doctorate from HGSE in Administration, Planning, and Social Policy and is a coauthor of *Finders and Keepers: Helping New Teachers Survive and Thrive in Our Schools* (2004).

Louise Kennedy is a reporter at the *Boston Globe* and the coauthor, with Linda K. Rath, of *The Between the Lions Book for Parents* (2004).

Reino Makkonen is an Education Pioneers 2004 Founding Fellow and a recent graduate of the Harvard Graduate School of Education. Makkonen compiled and edited *In Common*, the inaugural newsletter of the Coalition of Essential Schools. He previously served as the assistant editor of the *Harvard Education Letter*.

Katherine K. Merseth is the founding director of the School Leadership Program and director of the Teacher Education Program at the Harvard Graduate School of Education, where her work focuses on school leadership, teacher education, case method instruction, and mathematics education. She was also the founding executive director of the Harvard Children's Initiative, a university-wide program focusing on the needs of children. Merseth is editor of the book *Windows on Teaching: Cases of Secondary Mathematics Classrooms* (2003).

Robert Rothman is a principal associate at the Annenberg Institute for School Reform at Brown University. He has been a reporter and editor for *Education Week*, a senior project associate for Achieve, Inc., a study director for the National Research Council, and the director of special projects for the National Center on Education and the Economy. He is the author of *Measuring Up: Standards, Assessment and School Reform* (1995).

Alexander Russo is an independent education writer and a contributing editor for *Catalyst* magazine in Chicago. He is the editor of *School Reform in Chicago: Lessons in Policy and Practice*, published in 2004 by the Harvard Education Press.

Vivian Troen cofounded the Learning/Teaching Collaborative, one of the country's first professional development schools, and Trilemma Solutions, an education consultancy (www.trilemmasolutions.com). Troen is currently implementing professional development school initiatives at Brandeis University. She is coauthor (with K. C. Boles) of *Who's Teaching Your Children? Why the Teacher Crisis Is Worse Than You Think and What Can Be Done About It* (2003).

Debra Viadero is an associate editor at *Education Week*, where she writes primarily about education research. Her work has also appeared in *U.S. News & World Report*.

Index